THE BEST LOVED

# VILLAGES OF
# FRANCE

Written with the collaboration of Françoise Fonquernie

Translated from the French by David Radzinowicz
Design: Artimon, Gilles Ittel
Copyediting: Samuel Wythe
Typesetting: Thierry Renard
Proofreading: Sarah Kane
Color Separation: Reproscan, Lille
Printed in Slovenia by Florjancic Tisk

Originally published in French as *Les Villages préférés des Français*
© Flammarion, S.A., Paris, 2013
© Morgane Production, 2013

English-language edition
© Flammarion, S.A., Paris, 2014

This book is based on the television program
*Le Village préféré des Français*, broadcast by France Télévisions,
and created and produced by Morgane Production.

STÉPHANE BERN

# THE BEST LOVED
# VILLAGES OF
# FRANCE

Flammarion

# CONTENTS

# PREFACE

This book grew out of the extremely successful television series broadcast on France 2 Télévision in 2012 and 2013, *Le Village Préféré des Français*. It seeks to highlight the charm and magic of the best loved villages of France, and to testify to the country's scenic splendor. We spent two years crisscrossing the nation in search of forty-four villages that were representative of every region of France. In 2013, more than five million viewers watched Eguisheim in Alsace take first prize—a worthy successor to the previous year's winner, Saint-Cirq-Lapopie in the Midi-Pyrénées. The show's success, and the tide of interest it sparked in France's many villages—a good number of which could have justifiably claimed the coveted title themselves—is not hard to explain.

First and foremost, I believe that, by highlighting the incredible heritage of rural France—its history, its tourist sites, its architecture, and its wealth of welcoming residents—the series offered an overwhelmingly positive vision. I can honestly say that I would return from each village after a shoot with a deeper love for this beautiful country and its exceptional heritage. All of these little towns boast a remarkable history and numerous architectural treasures, but they also possess age-old traditions, often centered on their cuisine and their hearty way of life. This leads me to believe that a sense of togetherness, of conviviality, is not yet a thing of the past and is ever present in the villages of France. During these times of crisis and uncertainty, I understand the need of the French to return to their roots, to the soil, and to their regions: those comforting places that are the beating heart of France.

I, for one, have always enjoyed village life, with its relaxed approach to time, the rhythm of its seasons, and its respect for what the past has bequeathed. As I strolled through the villages of France while making this series, I also discovered how much a place's patrimony, its touristic appeal, and its cultural heritage can generate commercial activity. France is the foremost tourist destination in the world: it is both a public garden and an open-air museum. We should take advantage of this situation to increase employment in villages, where the way of life is so much more pleasant than in the outskirts of a city.

I took little persuading to join the project for this television show, produced by Morgane Production for France 2 Télévision, because I firmly believe that happiness is easier to find in close-knit towns than in the chilly anonymity of great cities, and, like all Parisians by adoption, I look back nostalgically on my village roots. In this era of globalization, with its frightening propensity to crush everything it cannot standardize, villages have an important role to play, both as guarantors of identity and as a creative force for the future. Moreover, it seems likely that local regions will acquire greater importance as the world becomes increasingly homogeneous and dislocated. To celebrate village life is also a positive act in the face of the current doom and gloom. There are real reasons to sing the praises of French villages, with their historical, cultural, and human heritage, and to extol the glories of a rural France that is neither a "dead museum," nor even an album of fading postcards, but a wonderful mosaic of riches that constitutes a national treasure.

I hope, dear readers, that you will derive as much pleasure as me from discovering the forty-four villages presented in this volume.

# ALSACE

ROUND EVERY CORNER, vineyards as far as the eye can see. Villages teeming with flowers invite the visitor to stay a while. With its half-timbered houses, peaceful forests, hills crowned with awe-inspiring fortresses, and towns where the welcome is always warm, Alsace boasts a richness and diversity that make it wonderfully attractive. It may be the smallest administrative region in France in terms of surface area, but its dynamism is evident. Above all a generous land, Alsace enjoys an enviable reputation for hospitality. Located on the banks of the River Rhine, on the borders of Switzerland and Germany, it bears the traces of a tumultuous history and shows a marked "European" sensibility. Its historical heritage is of the greatest interest, including such unforgettable monuments as Strasbourg Cathedral, the convent of Hohenbourg on Mont Saint-Odile, and an impressive concentration of strongholds and castles. The region has also made the most of its remarkable industrial past by setting up a large number of museums of technology, including two, dedicated to the train and the motor car, that are both favorites with visitors.

A land of art and culture, Alsace is still home to many craftsmen, notably ceramists who continue to ply their trade in villages such as Riquewihr. Alsatian cookery—with its succulent onion tart, *flammekueche* (a flambéed pie), fried carp, and gingerbread—has made its way to all four corners of the world. The Haeberlin family has become a household name, both father and son garnering countless culinary awards. Lastly, no one can visit Alsace without noticing the many storks and admiring the unique, traditional black bows that enhance the beauty of the local women.

*Facing page*: Right in the heart of the Alsace vineyards and the famous wine trail stands the attractive village of Riquewihr.

*Left*: Charming half-timbered houses, vineyards as far as the eye can see, storks' nests: three typical sights in the delightful region of Alsace.

# EGUISHEIM

"Take your partners, please!" In early June 2013, when Eguisheim was voted "France's Favorite Village" by tens of thousands of television viewers, its 1,611 inhabitants promptly invited everyone to join the party. If the television vote had taken place on May 19, the general jubilation would have been accompanied by due homage to St. Urban, patron saint of the region's wine-growers. A telling example of Eguisheim's deep-rooted respect for tradition, this annual festival takes the form of a colorful procession to the church of Saint-Pierre-et-Saint-Paul (whose bell tower dates to 1220), followed by Mass and a reception. Consistently awarded a national prize for its floral displays since 1989, recognized as one of the "Most Beautiful Villages of France" since 2003 by the association of the same name, and winner of a gold medal in the "European Competition for Towns and Villages in Bloom," this fortified village, founded in 1257, has more than its fair share of titles, but it well deserves this most recent accolade.

Along the wine trail about four miles (7 km) out of Colmar, at a bend in the road, there suddenly appears a cluster of roofs—a stone island floating in an ocean of vines. This is the village of Eguisheim, the birthplace of the vineyards of Alsace and the site of a medieval fortress built on an octagonal plan. The village's charm is obvious. Its lanes follow the layout of the stronghold's fortifications, arranged, like a maze, in concentric circles around the thirteenth-century castle. Built in pink sandstone, and still possessing stretches of ramparts, it gazes down proudly. The half-timbered dwellings of the winegrowers—some so small that they look like dollhouses—are all fitted with colored shutters. The village is awash with balconies, pointed gables, and wood-faced frontages brightened with abundant flowers. At the heart of the central square, the fountain of Saint-Léon has served the inhabitants faithfully; it is here that the Eguisiens would come to draw water

*Facing page*: In the center of the main square, the fountain of Saint-Léon recalls one of the village's most illustrious sons: St. Leo, a pope and a great traveler who strove for peace in Europe in the eleventh century.

*Left*: A celebration in the village of Eguisheim. This is the winemakers' festival, complete with costumed procession down the Grand'Rue.

*Above*: Window boxes on the lovely façade of a winemaker's house that now takes in guests.

*Pages 12–13*: Constructed in a series of concentric circles, the village of Eguisheim has the feel of a maze.

> *A marvelous village in Alsace that, with its pristine architectural integrity, amply deserves the title 'France's Favorite Village of 2013.'*

*Above, top*: Lined up on their wooden rack, *bretzels* resembling little bows await a customer. To bring out the taste, salt is sprinkled over the crust.

*Above, bottom*: Traditional half-timbered houses. In summer, flowers overflow from the balconies and window boxes.

*Facing page*: The Gothic bell tower of the church of Saint-Pierre-et-Saint-Paul, built in the fourteenth century. Inside, the wooden frame bears four bells, the largest hailing from the abbey at Marbach.

or to slake their animals' thirst. In 1880, it was surmounted by a statue of the saint, a native of the place
crowned pope in 1049. A nearby chapel devoted to his
memory guards a reliquary containing a fragment of his
skull. The medallions on the vault and the stained glass
recount various episodes in the saint's life. The inhabitants of the village are more than happy to tell the passing tourist everything about this jewel and seem to
delight in keeping it ship-shape.

Each year, spring ushers in a flurry of horticultural
activity, and whole families set to work all over the village. Here flowers are part and parcel of tradition, and
everybody is expected to get their hands dirty. "They
belong to our culture. We put them in window boxes
and on our front steps," Mélanie Gogniat informs us.
A "Friend of the Storks" will proudly invite you to look
up and observe the pairs of long-beaked birds perched
on the castle roof. "In the 1970s," observes M. Spiess,
one of the Friends, "the storks had deserted the village. A reintroduction program has brought them back.
'The Friends of the Storks' set up a marriage bureau
and business is on the up," he adds with a laugh. If by
chance there is no stork in the sky, look up anyway,
and decipher one of the sayings written on the lintel
of a house. Many are centuries old, and they are often
an appeal for divine protection. The most original in
essence declares: "What are you doing, staring at me?
On your way and mind your own business"!

A visit to Eguisheim would not be complete without
a crunchy pretzel (known here as *bretzel*), the best in
Alsace. If the recipe sounds like simplicity itself (flour,
water, sea salt), it calls for a surprising degree of dex-
terity. "You taper the edges, cross them, swap hands,
and then pull the short ends over the thick bit." Easier
said than done, and for beginners it is quite a challenge.
No matter. What you need to remember is that *bretzels*
should be eaten the day they are baked. In Eguisheim
they are recommended as an accompaniment to local
wines—in other words, wines from the slopes of the
Eichberg and the Pfersigberg, which are both classified
among Alsace's *grands crus*. Come evening, when the
shutters are closed, the visitor can sip a fine vintage in a
*winstub*, an Alsatian inn, to the sound of the accordion.

# RIQUEWIHR

Riquewihr must be one of the most delicious places on earth. Nestling at the entrance to a small, tree-clad valley on the Alsace plain, the village offers a splendid view over the valley of the Rhine, from the edges of the Alps to the fringes of the Vosges. Located eight miles (13 km) from Colmar and forty-three miles (70 km) from Strasbourg, encircled by vineyards, sheltered from the wind by three hills, and firmly on the Alsace wine route, this medieval city possesses an astonishing architectural heritage that has survived innumerable armed conflicts almost intact. Tragically, Riquewihr's historic center was struck by a violent accidental fire on January 1, 2014, which destroyed four houses and seriously damaged two others. It took five hours to contain the flames, as the layout of the medieval town complicated the firefighters' efforts.

One enters the village, which has preserved a stretch of its imposing fortified walls, by the Porte du Dolder (meaning, in Alsatian, "the highest point"). In the thirteenth century it was here that outsiders were checked and intruders repelled. Some eighty-two feet (25 m) high, the exterior façade of the towering belfry displays a military aspect, whereas the side facing the town is half-timbered and rises to four floors. Once the warder's lodging before being converted into the watch house,

*Right, top*: The ancient bell of the wine-loaders, at the top of the impressive Tour du Dolder, is rung at 5 a.m. and 10 p.m. each day.

*Right, bottom*: In Riquewihr, the typical Alsatian house reaches its acme, displaying every conceivable variety of carved timbering.

*Facing page*: Located right in the center of Alsace, the wine-producing village of Riquewihr is full of charm.

ANDRÉ HUGEL,
eighty-three years of age,
is chairman of Maison
Hugel et Fils, one of
the most famous wine
producers in Alsace.
But wine is not his only
passion: he is also a
history buff (and president
of the local history and
archaeology society). He
knows a tale about every
one of Riquewihr's streets
and houses, and proudly
describes the "Sainte-
Catherine" he keeps in his
cellar: the oldest wine
barrel in the world, dating
from the time of Louis XIV.

*Above*: In front of the Hugels' wine-
tasting center hangs a sign by Hansi,
a famous Alsatian artist.

*Facing page, top*: Spared during both
world wars, the village of Riquewihr
preserves its ancient charm.

*Facing page, bottom*: Behind the upper
gate, the village's medieval and
Renaissance architecture remains
almost entirely intact. Its paved streets
boast all kinds of architectural
splendors, rendered even more
attractive by an abundance of flowers.

Picturesque and admirably
preserved, it is also a rewarding
gastronomic stopover.

today the Dolder is the site of a museum that has been awarded special national status. Full of treasures, it tells the history of the fortified medieval village and of its evolution from the twelfth to the seventeenth centuries: its lords (the counts of Württemberg), its means of defense, and the occupants of its tower. A stone's throw from the Dolder, the Tour des Voleurs—a defensive structure dating to the beginning of the fourteenth century—used to serve as the seat of feudal justice at the time when Riquewihr belonged to Württemberg. The torture chamber (complete with strappado and oubliette) is open for visits, and the guardroom features a panoply of gruesome instruments. This "Tower of the Robbers" communicates with a sixteenth-century winegrower's house containing a kitchen strewn with historic utensils, a furnished bedroom, a cellar, and a storeroom where various tools recall the age-old crafts of the vine-tender and the cooper.

Riquewihr's upper gate preserves traces of the drawbridge that once protected the entrance. Its portcullis is one of the oldest in Europe, predating that in the Tower of London. Now installed in the former castle of the counts of Württemberg-Montbeliard, the Musée de la Communication en Alsace is the only one of its kind in France. Set up on the initiative of the Friends of the History of the Postal and Telecommunications Service in Alsace, and with the approval of the town council, the museum explains the story of long-distance communication since Gallo-Roman times, including the transportation of letters since the Middle Ages, when it was invented. Craftsmen—and in particular potters, who still turn their wheels in the open air—have long been a feature of this magnificent village. Visitors can take refreshment in interiors decorated in the solidly traditional style of the region. Local fare (*kougelhopf*, gingerbread, pretzels) is of course washed down with one of the excellent Alsatian wines, perhaps a Riesling. For those who wish to discover the wonders of Riquewihr from a different angle, there's the tourist train. After circling the village, it ends up in a vineyard offering an outstanding panorama.

# AQUITAINE

Beynac-et-Cazenac

Espelette

STRETCHING FROM THE ATLANTIC to the Pic du Midi, and from the banks of the Garonne to Spain, Aquitaine is a region where it feels good to be alive. Each of its five departments possesses its own strong identity. In the Dordogne, there are four Périgords: the Périgord Blanc lies around Ribérac and Brantôme, while the Périgord Noir stretches between the valleys of the rivers Vézère and Dordogne, and down to Sarlat, a town that knows its food. It is all started here, in the prehistoric cave of Lascaux. The meadows of the Périgord Vert spread out around Nontron and feed the "Blondes" of Aquitaine—the local cattle known for their fawn hide. The Périgord Pourpre encircles Bergerac, a town ever faithful to the cuisine of Gascony. In the Lot-et-Garonne, Agen, the prune capital, is also famous for its ancient aqueduct that allowed the barges of the region (called *gabarres*) to ferry produce down to the Gironde estuary. In Gironde, where wine is king, the Médoc extends along the left bank of the river, while Graves occupies the area south of Bordeaux and includes Sauternes, with its special microclimate. Gironde includes thirty-eight *appellations* and châteaux with evocative names. In Bordeaux, capital and economic hub rolled into one, where historic buildings stand cheek by jowl with fine contemporary architecture, trams glide noiselessly from the Gare Saint-Jean to the Place des Quinconces. At the opening of the Arcachon basin, the enormous Dune du Pilat offers unspoilted views: on one side, oyster beds and the Atlantic; on the other, the forests of the Landes. Standing among pines, the town of Dax owes its prosperity to its hot springs. Every village in the Landes organizes *courses landaises*, traditional bull-leaping competitions. The Basque Country boasts the superb beaches of Biarritz, Hossegor, Saint-Jean-de-Luz, and Guéthary. Henry IV of France was born in Pau in Béarn. Montaigne loved Aquitaine, as did Montesquieu, whose château at La Brède is open to the public. The books of François Mauriac, whose family resided in Malagar, are embedded in his native region.

*Facing page*: A *carrelet* in the Gironde estuary. The square net is lowered into the water from a hut built on piles. This style of fishing uses neither bait nor hook, but does rely on a modicum of luck.

*Left*: A string of fresh Espelette peppers; a team of free-range ducks; and the château of Saint-Geniès in the Périgord Noir. Aquitaine is a land of gastronomy, art, and history.

*Above*: From its rocky outcrop, Beynac-et-Cazenac's medieval castle peers down into the valley of the Dordogne, guarding the village.

*Facing page, left*: The west door of the church of Notre-Dame de l'Assomption, built within the castle's fortifications.

*Facing page, right*: Boats known as *gabarres* still sail down the Dordogne, as they always have. Now tourist craft, they offer the chance to explore the river's green and shady banks, with views of the imposing fortress above.

*Pages 24–25*: Aerial view of the castle at Beynac-et-Cazenac, taken from the plateau above.

# BEYNAC-ET-CAZENAC

Southwest of Sarlat, in the heart of the "black" Périgord and towering some 500 feet (150 m) above the Dordogne, is the village of Beynac-et-Cazenac. Pinned to a rock face dotted with caves, it stands, imperturbable, unchanging, watching over the quiet valley as it always has done. Dominated by its château, an austere-looking medieval pile and one of the best-preserved and most famous castles in the region, the village offers breathtaking views over the river below. Traditional *gabarres*—which have long contributed to the village's flourishing economy—still sail the river, but these days have been converted into pleasure craft. The cliff face being enough to discourage attacks from the river, the château's outworks face the plateau: they consist of double ramparts with battlements, a double moat (one of which is a natural ravelin), and a pair of barbicans guarding a large, square keep of Romanesque style. Abutting this stands a seigniorial house that was refurbished and enlarged in the sixteenth and seventeenth centuries. On the other side stands a further *logis*, partly dating from the fourteenth century, flanked by a courtyard and a staircase of square plan that serves the seventeenth-century apartments above, with their wood paneling and a period painted ceiling. The audience hall of the States of Périgord boasts a Renaissance fireplace carved with bucrania (ox skulls garlanded with flowers). This room gives onto a small oratory decorated in fresco. During the Hundred Years War, the Dordogne became a buffer zone between France and England; Beynac was one of the French strongholds, while not far off, on the other bank, the château of Castelnaud (which, along with Marqueyssac and Feyrac, is one of the three castles in the Dordogne's "golden triangle") remained in English hands. Richard the Lionheart laid waste to the area before perishing at a nearby castle. After the English had at last been driven out of Aquitaine, the castle remained in the same family until 1962, when it was purchased by Lucien Grosso, who dedicated all his

intelligence and enthusiasm to a restoration program lasting some fifty years.

Beynac-et-Cazenac is not confined to the heights, far from it: the village now sweeps down the hill to the banks of the river. Its steep lanes, bordered by houses with yellowish stone façades and roofs of round-edged, lapped stones called *lauzes*, are haunted by a thousand-year-old past and offer an enduring reminder of how our medieval ancestors lived. As in times gone by, the shutters of shopfronts open onto the street, displaying locally made foods and other articles. On the way up and on the way down, the visitor's mind keeps drifting back to days of yore, when peasants, weavers, basketmakers, fishermen and *gabarre* pilots would have filled the countryside and the banks of the Dordogne with hustle and bustle. It should not come as a surprise, then, to learn that many filmmakers have chosen this splendid medieval village as a backdrop for their movies, from *The Edifying and Joyous Story of Colinot*, Brigitte Bardot's last film made in 1973, to Luc Besson's *Joan of Arc* (1999).

The doyenne of the village, and its living database, is a lady called Renée, who ran the Hôtel Bonnet for sixty years. Now closed, this establishment saw its fair share of the great and the good, as testified by a visitor's book signed by Josephine Baker, Prince Charles, Brigitte Bardot, etc. However, history does not relate whether any of these luminaries was served a plate of *mique*, a Périgord specialty made of bread, eggs, flour, and oil, all soaked in vegetable stock and consumed piping hot. Television presenter Pierre Bellemare fell in love with this part of the Périgord some ten years ago, settling a few miles from Beynac: "There are some very, very beautiful villages, some real gems—but the jewel in the crown surely has to be Beynac." What fascinated him most was the local architecture: "You come back to the village a little like a tourist from the Middle Ages. There's not a single error of taste."

A little piece of heaven it may be, but Beynac-et-Cazenac is also a living entity inhabited by some six hundred hospitable Beynacois-et-Cazenacois, the lion's share of whom seem to meet up in the village bar for interminable and often noisy hands of *belote*. "I wouldn't move for anything in the world," says Daniel Doublier in his delight at belonging to this small community. The village also has a closely guarded secret of a geological, rather than gastronomical, nature. Down a little path hidden behind the castle are the caves of Redonduy.... But don't tell anyone!

From the town's cobbled lanes to the vast panorama over the valley of the Dordogne, the whole site is simply breathtaking.

*Facing page*: A steep lane bordered by houses of honey-colored stone roofed with *lauzes* (schist tiles).

*Top, left*: A cross engraved within a circle—perhaps dating from the time of the Templars.

*Top, right*: A lane climbing from the lower city to the castle.

*Bottom*: The houses reach all the way down to the water's edge, where the bathing and canoeing are excellent.

*Above*: At the foot of a mountain near the Basque coast and the Spanish border lies the colorful village of Espelette.

*Facing page, top*: The church of Saint-Étienne, a jewel of the Renaissance, boasts an impressive bell tower.

*Facing page, bottom*: A band performing a concert in front of the Hotel Euzkadi, where peppers are hung out to dry on the façade.

# ESPELETTE

Now *this* is a spicy village! September sees every house draped in a gown of "red gold." Hanging from garlands of wire several miles long, its harvest of blazing red peppers dries in the Basque Country sun. They are the pride of the village. "The peppers actually dry only in autumn. But they've become such an icon that they decorate the housefronts all year long," explains André Darraidou, born and bred in Espelette, where he served as mayor for seventeen years. He swears he'll never desert the place. "Looking at it, I often say to myself that those who wake up in the Champs-Élysées don't live better than we do. I love being in this place. There are so many beautiful houses to see, all so typical of the Labourd, my region," he adds.

André Darraidou always starts his walk in the area called Xerrenda, the site of the church of Saint-Étienne, one of the finest in the whole Basque Country. Since the seventeenth century, it has given rhythm to life in the town. For Espelettards, it is like a second home. "Here, much of life traditionally takes place in the church, accompanied by lovely ceremonies. When I was a child, everyone had their place. There wasn't really any obligation to do so, but people always sat in the same pew. Me, I was in the first gallery, to one side of the first pillar on the right, with my father on the other," our guide tells us. The second unmissable sight in the village is the wall used for Basque *pelote*, a lightning-fast ball game that combines strength and adroitness. It is still practiced by young locals, as are all the forms of the *force basque*, including tug-of-war. "One is harnessed to the same rope as one's adversary, and the aim is to pull him four meters. It doesn't matter how long it takes; it's the result that counts. Long ago, the game took place on the riverbank, the loser being dragged into the water," explains André, a man much attached, like everyone in Espelette, to the traditions that make

*Above*: The interior of the church of Saint-Étienne, with its three-storied gallery and masterly altarpiece.

*Right*: Picked by hand in the fields, peppers from Espelette have carried a label certifying their authenticity (*appellation d'origine contrôlée*) since 2000.

*Facing page, top*: A steep street lined with red-shuttered houses in typical Basque style.

*Facing page, bottom*: Blazing garlands of peppers drying on a balcony in the warm Basque sun.

It is *the* typical Basque village: welcoming, proud, full of customs and traditions. Don't miss the Espelette pepper festival at the end of October.

up the vibrant identity of the village. The third stop is the cemetery, in front of the pink marble Art Deco tomb belonging to Agnès Souret, who lived in the village and who, in 1920, was elected the first Miss France. To repatriate her body from Argentina, where this dazzlingly beautiful girl died of peritonitis in 1928, her mother had to sell the family home. Another native of Espelette, and a very different personality, was Armand David (1826–1900): a Lazarist priest, and eminent zoologist and botanist, who discovered the rare giant panda in eastern Tibet, among other species.

Returning to the "spice village," we stop off at Marixu's, one of fifty producers of the condiment synonymous with the name of Espelette that has earned the village worldwide fame. It was the Spanish who brought this red fruit, which since 2000 comes with a guarantee of authenticity, over from Colombia and Mexico in the fifteenth century. From Spain, the plant hopped over to Labourd in the Basque Country, where it encountered ideal growing conditions around Espelette. At Marixu's, one can taste some of the finest *piment d'Espelette* in the area. As André Daraidou comments, with his characteristic flair for poetry: "It reminds me of how peppers used to taste. The tip of the tongue is highly sensitive to tangy tastes—but on the middle of the tongue it develops a gradual, rich pungency. I feel tears welling up ...

tears of emotion." The current president of Biarritz Olympique, Serge Blanco—one of the most-capped French rugby players, with ninety-three appearances in the national team to his credit, and now an experienced businessman—continues in the same vein: "It has an inimitable taste that brings out and enhances the taste of food, including chocolate. Chocolate with Espelette pepper is a real treat, like so many other by-products: preserves, candies, jellies, creams, oils, vinegars, perfumes.... Each bears the stamp of Espelette and of the Basque Country. This is our bounty, and it works such wonders in the guts that it can't be put into words. There are only glances—glances and songs that transport you to another world."

# AUVERGNE

IN THE HEART OF FRANCE, between the Cantal and the Allier, the Auvergne is a land of wide-open spaces and now dormant volcanoes. The air is as pure as the tinkle of a *clarine* bell on a cow in summer pasture. Water flows in abundance, and the fauna and flora are carefully preserved. The regional nature reserve of the Volcans d'Auvergne includes more than a hundred vents that long ago spat out miles of lava and tons of rock. Known as *puys*, they form neat rows, and their summits—topped by great craters— offer exceptional vistas. At the heart of the chain of mountains, nine miles (15 km) from the city of Clermont-Ferrand, Vulcania, a scientific amusement park, tells you everything you could wish to know about the bowels of the earth.

In the vast calm of the Livradois-Forez nature reserve, the visitor can overdose on clean air and the smells of nature. The park's variations in altitude and climate mean that eagle owls live alongside otters and other endangered species. With eyes peeled and ears pricked, you might find traditional crafts and innovative industries thriving in the middle of the countryside, as well as museums, castles, and other locations marked by history: Ambert, the land of Fourme cheese and a papermaking town; Thiers, which hugs its hillside, the cutlers' capital; and Châteldon, where a health-giving mineral water gushes from its source between two rocks.

Auvergne owes its name to the Arverni tribe, whose king, from 52 BCE, was Vercingetorix. Absorbed into the fledgling French kingdom at an early date, it was also the birthplace of Lafayette, who grew up in the château of Chavaniac-Lafayette. Dominated by the Volvic gray stone, the larger metropolitan area of Clermont-Ferrand houses one-third of the region's population. Wedged between two hills, Clermont serves as headquarters for many international companies, mostly in the sectors of pharmaceuticals and tire manufacture. The tire giant Michelin, for example, has always had its registered office in the city.

*Facing page*: Close to Orcines, in the middle of the Volcans d'Auvergne regional park, the summit of the awesome Puy Pariou contains two craters, one nestling within the other. The Puy de Dôme is visible less than a mile away.

*Left*: Saint-Nectaire, in the Monts Dore mountain range, huddles around a Romanesque church. The surrounding area has lent its name to an excellent cheese made from the milk of Salers cows, herds of which graze below the castle of Anjony, with its four fifteenth-century round towers.

# BLESLE

One hour from Clermont-Ferrand, in the hollow of a valley in deepest Auvergne, lies a jewel: Blesle, a unique, exceptional, extraordinary village. It is an excellent place to bring up a family. It gets under your skin, and its effect is almost tangible. Actor and presenter Gérard Klein is a prime example. For a time a pub landlord and a stockbreeder, owning about fifty Salers cattle in the village, he still returns as often as he can to spend time with his buddies. "This region, this village bewitched my wife and our daughters, who spent their childhood here. Now they've grown up and have lives of their own we've moved on, but they often come back. You can't shrug off Blesle just like that," he observes, as his old pal Paul, the parish priest, offers him a heartfelt welcome.

The history of the town is etched into the stones of the Catholic church. It all began at the end of the ninth century, with the foundation of the Benedictine convent of Saint-Pierre by Ermengard of Auvergne. (Ermengard was the mother of William the Pious, duke of Aquitaine and the founder of the great abbey of Cluny.) Indeed, it was the convent's abbess who was the *seigneur* of the village—a state of affairs of which the barons of Mercoeur disapproved. Deciding to take it over, they encroached on the rights of the abbey and sparked a feudal war. In spite of repeated protests from the abbesses, the barons erected a castle with an imposing tower reinforced by two buttresses, today known as the "Tower with Twenty Corners." In the twelfth century, the abbey church was reconstructed and given two apsidal chapels and a chancel larger than the nave. The cloistered nuns now occupied houses giving onto the convent's inner court. In the fourteenth century, owing to a rise in population, an additional church was erected.

*Facing page*: Two figurative corbels, somewhat different from the traditional themes found in the church architecture of the Basse-Auvergne. In the central image, a house's wooden shutters have two heart-shaped openings that allow in the daylight but keep the occupants safe from prying eyes. These examples have been sensitively restored, although many others have disappeared.

*Above*: Although it was initially intended to serve a convent, this Romanesque church, built between 849 and 885, was dedicated to St. Peter on the authorization of Pope Urban II.

*Right, top*: Set deep within the surrounding stonework, the carved doorway, wrought-iron knocker, and nail-studded planks testify to Blesle's medieval past.

*Right, bottom*: A coat of arms above the entrance to the old hospital, which was erected in the sixteenth century, where pilgrims and other patients were treated for free. It depicts the scallop-shell symbol of St. James and two pilgrims' staffs. The date of 1622 commemorates the fact that four villagers completed the pilgrimage to Santiago de Compostela that year.

*Above*: Dozens of half-timbered houses with tiled roofs remind the visitor of Blesle's long history.

*Left*: Restoration works at the church of Saint-Pierre, completed in 2009, have returned the chancel's wall paintings to their former glory. Such opulent decoration testifies to the importance of the abbey and its church.

*Facing page*: The bell tower of Saint-Martin. The church itself, built in the fourteenth century, was destroyed in 1793.

From this glorious, if turbulent, period there remain an enclosing wall, some towers, two churches, forty-three weatherboard houses, various carved doors, and little byways that wander down to the river. The Voireuze river, which meanders between the Matalou and town bridges, and passes under that belonging to the "sisters," is flanked by washhouses and attractive gardens. It serves as the starting point for no fewer than seventeen walking trails. A museum of headwear (the Musée de la Coiffe) has been set up in the sixteenth-century former hospital—where pilgrims and beggars were treated for free—displaying some seven hundred caps, bonnets, hats, and ribbons as worn in Auvergne from the late eighteenth to the end of the twentieth century.

> The villagers should be congratulated for their titanic efforts. They have restored more than forty-three timber-clad houses and returned them to their former glory.

Blesle may have turned its back on the hustle and bustle of the wider world, but it is far from asleep. Determined to publicize their little medieval town and to keep its heart beating, the 650 inhabitants have done much to valorize its architectural splendor and rapturous scenery. The Bleslois are renowned for their warmth, as Gérard Klein attests: "I recall one old lady, a Mme Segrey, whom everyone here called 'Zezette.' She played the organ and had us in stitches. At the end of the piece or the service she'd get up and ask: 'You want more?' We all guffawed. I've always found the church delightful and the village truly warm-hearted."

Pascal, the mayor, comes up. The church and the town hall face one another like something from the Don Camillo stories, just as they did during the age of the Mercoeurs and the abbey: the two mainstays of the community. "Eh well, it's not often you walk by the church so early in the morning," the "Don Camillo" of Blesle observes to his "Peppone." And the mayor replies, all smiles: "Well, no, actually. I had to work late last night. Council meeting, you understand." If they often tease one another, the two men enjoy a mutual respect, working, each in his way, for the commune, as Mimi, long a feature of the village, assures us. In another life, she was an army commander, before buying a house here that she has painstakingly restored.

Blesle even possesses its own anthem that Blésois belt out at get-togethers and village festivities. It was composed by Jean Sarrus, onetime member of a famous French band, who has settled here. "Elle est vraiment Blesle [belle], la vie," goes the chorus.

# SALERS

An Auvergne *bourrée* is being danced on the village square. A few tourists, including sprinter Marie-Jo Perec, who is just passing through, are invited to get to their feet. And one, two, three, in time with the accordion and the *cabrette* bagpipes. It's partytime in Salers—as it so often, especially in the summer. This splendid village, nominated one of the "Most Beautiful Villages of France," sits on a basalt hill high above the valley of the Maronne in the Volcans d'Auvergne regional nature reserve, beside an old lava flow and well off the main transport routes.

On account of the village's relative isolation and its rugged winters, it has remained small in size, though this has not prevented it from becoming famous throughout the world and attracting 300,000 visitors a year. In 1950, *Paris Match* took a photograph of a girl staying in the only campsite in the area rinsing her linen in a wash-house. The girl in the *lavoir* was Jacqueline Bouvier, the future Jackie Kennedy. In May 2010, the Hungarian village of Hollokö, a UNESCO World Heritage Site, was twinned with this pearl of the Cantal. At the official ceremony, the coats-of-arms of each borough were tilted toward each other, just as at weddings between noble families in times gone by.

Once a baronetcy, Salers (the final "s" is silent) is set like a jewel in the surrounding pastureland—the "medieval hill city" celebrated in the Occitan language by local poet Arsène Vermenouze. Philippe Garrigue, a descendant of the La Ronade family, which has provided several civil magistrates to the bailiwick of Salers, is our guide and a walking encyclopedia. Along the way, our blueblood Sagranier (as the inhabitants of Salers are called) soaks his audience in the atmosphere of this historic village lying at the foot of the mountain. To the great pleasure of his listeners, Philippe takes his time. He obviously adores Salers

*Above*: The Place Tyssandier d'Escous in Salers. On the left is the fifteenth-century Maison du Bailliage; on the right, the Maison de Flogeac, built a century later. Together, they demonstrate the astonishing architectural integrity of this village of lava stone and *lauze* roofs.

*Facing page, top*: The Maison du Commandeur (the so-called "Templars' House"), with its superb arcaded corridor, now houses a museum of the village's folklore and traditions.

*Facing page, bottom*: Salers cheese maturing in the cellar of the Nouaille dairy. Salers is a cow's-milk cheese with a firm texture and thick rind, whose authenticity is carefully protected.

and is proud of it. The houses, stores, and restaurants here are built out of volcanic rock. He himself lives in the oldest house in the village: the Hôtel de la Ronade, whose foundations date back to the thirteenth century. Towering over the main square, it extends over three floors. Its owner readily opens some of the rooms in this listed building to visitors, as well as staging literary evenings organized by "The Friends of Salers." Philippe leads you to the fifteenth-century belfry looming over the main shopping street, then down the Rue

66 Salers is a country of red cows, cheese, and, above all, medieval splendor and superb views over the valleys. 99

*Left, top*: The Porte du Beffroi, also called the "Clock Gate," is a square tower surmounted by an ironwork bell-cot. The bell sounds every half hour.

*Left, bottom*: With its long, curly, dark mahogany coat, and slender but impressive horns, a Salers bull watches jealously over its pasture and its herd.

*Above*: The village of Salers emerges above the surrounding pastureland. With the mountains of the Auvergne on the distant horizon, this bucolic scenery attracts many visitors and walkers.

des Nobles by the Maison du Bailliage toward the Rue des Templiers, where there's a museum dedicated to historic furniture and period costumes. Rather unexpectedly, this museum also houses an abstract piece by the polemical author Jean-Edern Hallier, a friend of the local solicitor. Halting in front of the last remaining ramparts at the Porte de la Martille, Philippe then shows you the Renaissance-fronted village hall on the Place Tyssandier d'Escous. The square is dedicated to an agronomist who did much to give the cows of Salers the reputation they enjoy today by rejuvenating the breed; his statue stands at its center. Splendid cattle with a fiery coat, russet ringlets around the muffle, and lyre-shaped horns, Salers are raised both for their meat and their milk, and they are the inhabitants' pride and joy. From May to October, they are moved up to summer pasture. With its aroma of high-grown grass, their unctuous milk is used in making the excellent cheese that bears their name, whose flavor is much enhanced when consumed with some oven-baked bread.

There's no actual farm in the village. Farmsteads are dotted around the surrounding hamlets of Jarriges, La Jourdanie, and Le Mouriol (this last hosts the municipal campsite and a hotel complex). Some of the livestock farms, such as the one on which Antoine works, are open to visitors. Antoine, a true son of the land, still loves to stroll about his village. Once his work is finished, he is generally to be found in the company of Alphonse and Robert, *boule* in hand, on the Esplanade de Barrouze that dominates the valley of the Maronne and the Puy Violent. Fingering the *cochonnet* (the little ball that serves as the target), these tireless players of *pétanque* also throw the odd glance over the exceptional panorama they have lived with since boyhood. Even better is to see it from a hot-air balloon. "Ah! What a view you get over the Auvergne when you leave the landlubbers behind. Yep, there's no denying that," they exclaim. Always ready with sound advice, the Sagraniers are a jovial bunch who take the time to live and who like to share a laugh. That's surely enough to make the village worth a visit.

# BASSE-NORMANDIE

Barfleur

La Perrière

LESS THAN 130 MILES (200 km) from Paris, the landscapes of Basse-Normandie present a splendid palette of green. The Pays d'Auge is planted with apple orchards; the Cotentin is full of copses and marshland; in the Perche there are forests. Everywhere Normandy cows chew the cud in verdant pastures, and in the area surrounding Ouche there are horses. To the north and west of this bountiful land, the sea crashes against cliffs and washes fine-sand beaches along 290 miles (470 km) of coastline. Chic seaside resorts lie along the shore where the light and color inspired the Impressionists. Comprising three departments, Basse-Normandie occupies the western part of the former province of Normandy and the north of the county (*comté*) of the Perche. Heaving with history and tradition, today it is also a leisure destination, served by major railway lines and the Paris-Caen-Octeville-Cherbourg road. From meadows to beaches (some of which were used for the D-Day landings), Calvados—the birthplace of William the Conqueror—is perfect for rambling in all seasons. The Pays d'Auge, with its manors and half-timbered houses, starts in Deauville and includes the area around Lisieux; it is dedicated to the horse, and houses several famous stud farms and riding schools. Including the bay of Mont-Saint-Michel (a UNESCO World Heritage Site) and Granville, a onetime buccaneering town from which boats left to fish for cod in Newfoundland, the Manche coastline is known for its islands, beaches, groves, and marshes. All vale and dale, the Orne is literally the high point of Normandy. At more than 1,300 feet (413 m), the Signal d'Écouves overlooks the forest of the same name to the north of Alençon, the department's county town and, since the seventeenth century, the acknowledged "queen of lace."

*Facing page*: Dotted with sturdy apple trees, the green pastures around Livarot are grazed by cows that provide some of the finest milk in the world.

*Left*: The wide beaches of Cotentin are often used for equine thalassotherapy, a treatment that has made great progress over the last few decades; a half-timbered house typical of the Pays d'Auge; the beach at Barneville-Carteret is sheltered by the dunes and cliffs that overlook the English Channel.

# BARFLEUR

At the tip of the Cotentin peninsula, seventeen miles (28 km) from Cherbourg, Barfleur spins out its peaceful days in rhythm with the tides. A fishing village of subtle charm, it was much loved by the painter Paul Signac and more recently has won the favors of one of France's most voluble food critics, who has had a house here for twenty years. Jean-Luc Petitrenaud is a self-confessed fan of this port, from where (legend has it) King Arthur set out to fight the Romans in present-day Savoy. "There is a softness in its pastel colors and the roughness of its stone. With the church on the left and Rue Saint-Nicolas on the right, one is at the heart of village life the second one enters. It's really tiny. All told, Barfleur has six hundred inhabitants," its adoptive son declares.

Pocket-sized it certainly is. Covering just 143 acres (58 hectares), Barfleur is the smallest commune in all the Manche, but that doesn't stop it being charming and picturesque. An ancient port long open to England and Northern Europe, it offers a convenient and practical stopover for boats undertaking short trips at sea and yachts plying between France and England or sailing over to the Channel Islands. Access is facilitated by a port lock, and it provides good anchorage. It feels good, too, to stroll along its flowery terraces and down bustling lanes lined by granite houses, some of which date back several centuries: they are sober, solid, uniform, and comfy-looking to the portside, while a little farther on the fishermen's tenements are more modest but just as engaging.

*Facing page, left*: An elegant glazed earthenware finial crafted by two Barfleur potters, Patrick Lefebvre and Ingrid Guilbert.

*Facing page, right*: Affixed to a boulder at the port entrance, this plaque recalls how, in 1066, William the Conqueror set sail from Barfleur to invade England.

*Above*: The port at high tide. Ideally positioned for traffic to England and Northern Europe, it offers a stopover for boats on short crossings and for yachts plying the coasts.

The harbor is charming. Trawlers
and pleasure boats moor alongside quays
laden with lobster pots and *blondes,*
Barfleur's famous mussels.

The dock is often busy with
trawlers unloading their cargo
of fish and mussels, the famous
*blondes de Barfleur.* As often
as he can, food critic Jean-Luc
Petitrenaud waits for them
on the quayside.

Sea breezes have left their mark on all the buildings here, and every winter leaves deeper traces. If you carry on to the end of the port you come across the house where author Jules Renard stayed in 1890, built on top of the old fort destroyed in 1597. In his work, Renard describes the lighthouse in nearby Gatteville, reached down a narrow, winding road. At a height of 246 feet (74.9 m), it is the second tallest in Europe. Now automated and fitted with xenon lamps, for centuries it has warned of the fierce currents at the headland that have caused so many shipwrecks. These conditions also explain why the first lifeboat station in France, built in 1865 on the British model, appeared at Barfleur. Over the years it has been equipped with six boats, the first three being powered by oarsmen. The last—the *Amiral de Tourville*, launched in 1997—can still be seen, docked amid the fishing vessels. The first lifeboat, meanwhile—the *Crestey et Sauvé*—is displayed

INGRID GUILBERT AND PATRICK LEFEBVRE
(here with Jean-Luc Petitrenaud, in the center)
are master ceramists. They have lived in Barfleur
for several decades, and their wares are displayed
on almost every slate- or schist-roofed house
in the village, including ridge tiles, finials,
door numbers, and street signs.

*Above, bottom*: A boat arrives
back in port on the Quai Henri
Chardon. The deck is laden
with bags of mussels collected
between the headlands
at Barfleur and Saire.

*Facing page, top*: The Gatteville
lighthouse at Barfleur warns
of strong currents just off the
coast. The tower has as many
steps as there are days
in the year.

*Facing page, bottom*: The blue
front door and matching
shutters of a local cottage. As
if to symbolize an entire way of
life, a trug of oysters or mussels
is tied on the back of the bicycle.

under a shelter close to the church, together with many documents recording heroic rescues.

A stroll through the village is a journey back in time. The Cour Sainte-Catherine preserves its squat-looking fifteenth-century houses. In the port, fixed into the rock, a plaque recalls how William the Conqueror left for England in 1066 on a longship, the *Mora*, piloted by Étienne, a young man from Barfleur. It was William, already duke of Normandy, who would take over the English throne. In 1120, however, a royal launch, the *Blanche-Nef*, sank off the coast of Barfleur with the son of Henry I on board—an unfortunate circumstance that heralded the decline of ducal interest in the harbor. In the mid-fourteenth century, townsfolk gathered at the church—at that time in the middle of the town—to watch helplessly as English troops under Edward III devastated the surrounds. Today, owing to coastal erosion, the church is on the shoreline. Near the end of World War II, on June 24, 1944, American troops liberated Barfleur without a shot being fired, converting it into a supply yard for the Allies.

Portside is the only place to be when the ships come in. There you can buy spray-fresh fish, as well as delicious *blondes de Barfleur*—a type of wild mussel greatly prized for its taste and plump flesh. As you walk about, don't forget to look up, because there is much to see above head height. Elaborate glazed-terracotta finials crown roofs of schist and attic windows, lending a brighter touch to a color scheme dominated by gray: symbols of wealth, they proclaim the owner's prosperity from the rooftops.

# LA PERRIÈRE

Perched on a rocky outcrop on the fringes of the forest of Bellême, La Perrière benefits from unparalleled views over the scenery of the Perche and the woodland of Perseigne and Écouves. A onetime episcopal retreat, this village of three hundred souls sixteen miles (26 km) from Alençon boasts a bishop's residence: an imposing thirteenth-century masonry house with a square tower formerly used as a dungeon. Halfway between the Paris Basin and the massif of Brittany, in the heart of the natural park of Le Perche, La Perrière was a stopping place for pilgrims on the road to Mont Saint-Michel.

With its characteristic houses, built in an iron-rich stone (*pierre de roussard*) that constitutes one of its chief attractions, and its manicured gardens, the village has been dubbed the "pearl of the Perche." "It was no foregone conclusion," explains Claude, who used to be a grocer here: "Just thirty years ago, these splendid stones were not highly thought of. People were not above covering them in render to hide them. They

weren't much liked and were thought an eyesore. But everything comes from the soil of La Perrière. And it's quite lovely." The recent transformation was due to the "Parisians," as the locals call them. It was they who revamped the houses, highlighting the quality of the beautiful stonework, previously neglected.

One of these "Parisians" was the fashion designer Chantal Thomass: "La Perrière has a great deal of charm; it's a pretty village. There are beautiful buildings, beautiful manor houses—and," she notes, "it's not that far from Paris." She is especially delighted by the village's interest in art and in its artist outreach days. On the occasion of the art market, held every year on Pentecost weekend, a hundred artists exhibit in the street and in cellars, barns, and gardens. Contemporary art occupies the whole village, turning it into an uplifting, bustling place. If you need to take the weight off your feet, you could do worse than make your way to the Maison d'Horbé, presided over by chef Laurent Loingtier. Here you can taste tidbits in an interior decorated with all kinds of antiques.

*Facing page*: From a hill on the outskirts of the forest of Bellême, La Perrière gazes down on the meadows, woodland, and sunken lanes of the Perche countryside.

*Left*: The Maison d'Horbé, on the village's most attractive square, is a restaurant-cum-antiques store.

Locals and newcomers came together to make this event possible and decided to live here in harmony, as Julien Cendres confirms. The author discovered La Perrière twenty-five years ago: "I had a kind of revelation, up on the spur. I had the sense there was something unique here, something really powerful. I felt I just had to move in here." Everyone he has met has been friendly, and now their pride in the village is his, too. The Percheron, a draft horse capable of drawing mail coaches, carriages, omnibuses, and other vehicles, is another source of local pride. Sidelined by the arrival of the motorcar, these broad-chested, powerful animals are still seen in harness ambling through nearby park- or woodland, such as the forest of Bellême, an immense domain whose oaks famously supplied masts for vessels of the royal fleet. One especially well-known specimen, the "Chêne de l'École," was planted in 1666 during the reign of Louis XIV and now stands 138 feet (42 m) high, with a circumference of 15 feet (4.6 m). Having survived the centuries, its great trunk is worth examining. In 1927, the tree was dedicated to the national forestry and waterways school.

Having learned of its existence from the writer Julien Cendres, Chantal Thomass became interested in a rapidly vanishing embroidery technique developed in the early nineteenth century by the women of the village: beaded netting, which they used to run up into drapes. The Perche was at that time an important manufacturing center, whose products were dispatched to Paris, Rouen, Britain, and the United States. "Bead netting has this thoroughly modern, pared-down, clean-lined look," the lingerie designer informs us. Under her auspices, and based on research undertaken by a local lady, Mme Lethon, this netting technique has been given a new lease of life and is being taken up elsewhere.

A true rural town,
full of colorful houses,
in a region I'm particularly
fond of. As a recent resident
of the Perche, I love
the traditional character
of these villages.

*Facing page, left*: A secondhand store specializing in small pieces of furniture and kitchenware.

*Facing page, right*: One of the many beautiful gardens in La Perrière.

*Above, top*: Behind this pretty terrace of ocher-colored housefronts, the Maison de la Mode d'Antan and the Maison du Filet have been converted into a pair of museums that perpetuate the net-making traditions of La Perrière, which have gained a new lease of life under the impetus of lingerie designer Chantal Thomass.

*Above, bottom*: Hiring a carriage pulled by Percheron horses is an excellent way to appreciate the local countryside.

# BURGUNDY

Flavigny-sur-Ozerain
Vézelay

A LAND OF TRADITION and fine food, Burgundy (or Bourgogne) is sited on a major river and important road links between France and the rest of Europe. This economic and cultural hub is practically an open-air history book. This region, just an hour from Paris by high-speed train, witnessed some of the greatest events in the annals of France, from the Battle of Alésia, where Vercingetorix held firm against Julius Caesar, to the foundation of the Benedictine abbey at Cluny in the tenth century—one of the most important spiritual and intellectual centers on the continent. A powerful duchy that resisted the kingdom of France before finally joining forces with it, Burgundy abounds in architectural treasures: medieval villages such as Semur-en-Auxois and Flavigny, and amazing castles including Cormatin and Pierreclos in Saône-et-Loire, and Tanlay in the Yonne. The entire region can be crossed on water, and you can also wend your way down the narrow Burgundy canal connecting the Seine Basin to the Rhône, tying up at Tonnerre to explore the nature reserve of the Morvan. Then, to the south of Auxerre, climbers can scale the impressively rugged cliffs of the Saussois. Farther on, at 1,614 feet (492 m) high, the Roche de Solutré offers unimpeded views over vines, villages, and woodland.

Burgundy is no stranger to gastronomic pleasures. Charolais beef in the region's famous *boeuf bourguignon*, Époisses cheese, Dijon mustard, great wines such as Romanée Conti—all make it paradise on earth for those in search of fine food. From November 1 to 12 every year, Dijon, its capital, with its ducal palace and its ancient streets lined with mansions and their towering porches, holds an international food fair that is one of the biggest in France. Beaune and its hospices present the finest bottles of Côte de Nuits, Clos de Vougeot, and Chablis in the kind of festive atmosphere adored by the Burgundians, who have a talent for the arts and for pleasure—and even for both, simultaneously.

*Facing page*: The vineyard and château of Clos Vougeot in the fall.

*Left*: The vineyard at Mâcon Lugny in springtime; a rare example of medieval civic architecture, the Hospices de Beaune is roofed in brightly colored glazed tiles that form geometric shapes; on the Nivernais canal, a visitor drifts past the cliffs of the Saussois, a popular center for rock climbing.

# FLAVIGNY-SUR-OZERAIN

No medieval town could be more "foodie" than Flavigny-sur-Ozerain. Since the eighth century it has sold aniseed candies made to a recipe perfected in 719 by the Benedictines of the abbey of Saint-Pierre, and it has now gained national recognition for this remarkable heritage. Known all over the world, today these candies are even exported to China.

If you approach the village from the road that connects it to Semur-en-Auxois, you arrive at Flavigny from the side, beneath its rocky outcrop. The remains of the enclosing wall chiseled out against the sky betray a medieval stronghold. Occupying a green hill at the meeting point between three rivers—the Ozerain, the Brenne, and the Verpant—the light-toned masonry and red-tiled roofs of Flavigny exude a charm typical of many Burgundian villages. Entering by the Porte du Bourg, a gate long ago deprived of its drawbridge, you stumble immediately across respectable residences with staircase turrets and mullioned windows, and houses with shopfronts that once belonged to tanners, oil-sellers, millers, tinsmiths, glassmakers, weavers, and winegrowers—a long-vanished world that here suddenly comes back to life.

The narrow, sometimes steep lanes remind the visitor how this remote settlement was essentially dedicated to defense and prayer. "These alleyways form a passive defense system," explains Gérard, a resident for whom Flavigny has no secrets. "When the enemy encroached in large numbers, the defenders would draw them into these lanes that are so narrow that only one man-at-arms could pass at a time. They just had to wait and then whack them over the head, one after another. An entire company could be dispatched like that."

*Facing page*: Constructed in a light-colored stone and capped with red-tiled roofs, the town's houses have preserved many of their original staircase turrets and mullioned windows.

*Left*: At Flavigny-sur-Ozerain, the famous aniseed candies for which the village is renowned are still made. The recipe was perfected in 719 by the abbey's Benedictine monks.

CATHERINE TROUBAT makes the famous local aniseed candies, like three generations of her family before her.

The telltale sweetish odor of aniseed makes it hard to ignore Flavigny's principal trade for the last thousand years. "When the monks fled during the Revolution, the people of the village took over the abbey like squatters, and they've continued to make candy here ever since," Catherine Troubat tells us. Since 1923, three generations of Troubats, aided by a staff of thirty, have overseen the manufacture and sale of various aniseed delicacies to the tune of about 250 tons a year. To visit the workshops you just have to pop on a hairnet and follow the guide.

A little higher up the village, people huddle around the doorway of a farmhouse-cum-inn that is always bursting at the seams. There, some fifteen years ago, a group of farmers' wives, feeling cut off in their farmsteads, decided to join up to cook and sell their produce. Thus La Grange aux Femmes was born, and it was a great hit with locals and tourists alike. You can combine your meal with a walk around the storehouses packed with wines made from no fewer than six grape varieties: Aligoté, Chardonnay, Auxerrois,

Pinot Beurot, Pinot Noir, and César, all grown in the surrounding area. You might want to continue with a visit to the Maison des Arts Textiles et du Design, founded by designer Daniel Algranate, whose grounds have a botanical garden devoted to plants employed in textile manufacture.

Flavigny's keynote is authenticity. Miss France 2013, Burgundy's own Marine Lorphelin, is not one to be ashamed of her native region, and she tells everyone who cares to listen how they must come to see it for themselves. Certain filmmakers have gone one better and used the village as a set. So it was that a good number of Flavigny's 347 inhabitants appeared as extras in Lasse Hallström's film *Chocolat*, starring Juliette Binoche and Johnny Depp.

Flavigny-sur-Ozerain is slowly losing one of its idiosyncrasies, however. Up until recently, the postman had to deliver the mail without the benefit of house numbers. But the authorities have now had their way, and numbers have started appearing.

The aniseed candies are world famous, but the town's architectural heritage also makes it worth a visit.

*Facing page*: An advertising poster for Flavigny's most famous produce. Dispensing machines in stations and subways have sold the bonbons since 1923.

*Above*: Flanked by two round towers, the Porte du Val is the gate by which one entered the town's fortifications. Although it has long disappeared, one can easily imagine the noise made by the massive portcullis as it crashed down on unwanted visitors.

*Right*: The Benedictine abbey's Carolingian crypt now houses the factory where the candies are made. The place is suffused with the captivating smell of confectionery.

# VÉZELAY

Vézelay's main attraction is the meditative atmosphere of the basilica of Sainte-Marie-Madeleine. Located 150 miles (240 km) from Paris, atop one of the last hills before the end of the Morvan, this jewel of Romanesque art restored by Viollet-le-Duc has watched over the village since the twelfth century. An important pilgrimage center and a UNESCO World Heritage Site since 1979, the basilica towers over a medieval settlement of 450 inhabitants, where some of the narrow, winding streets date back to the fifteenth century. The church is approached from the main street lined with houses whose cellars open directly onto the sidewalk. Tourists come in droves to follow in the footsteps of some great writers: Georges Bataille, René Char, Paul Éluard, Paul Claudel, and Romain Rolland all chose to reside here and to climb the "Inspired Hill." It is indeed an inspirational place: listening to a four-voiced polyphonic Vespers sung by the monks and nuns of the Fraternity of Jerusalem is an intensely emotional experience. If you ask the Very Reverend François Tricart, proctor of the basilica and its current overseer, why people have been coming to Vézelay for a thousand years, he invariably answers: "Because of Mary Magdalene." Relics of the saint and disciple of Jesus have been preserved here since the eleventh century.

*Above, left*: The carvings at Vézelay inspire a mood of serenity.

*Above, right*: Clad in white, three nuns of the monastic Order of Jerusalem pray during one of the three daily services celebrated in Vézelay's basilica.

*Facing page*: The basilica's nave is 205 feet (63 m) long and 61 feet (19 m) high. The round arches of the vault are made of alternating white and brown stones.

Pages 62–63: At the summit of a hill in the Morvan, the basilica of Sainte-Marie-Madeleine—now awarded UNESCO World Heritage status—has stood guard over the village of Vézelay since the twelfth century.

Above, top: Paved in cobbles and bordered by old houses, the Rue de la Bonnette is one of the most charming in the village.

Above, bottom: The abbey's crypt, which lies beneath the chancel, dates from the Carolingian era.

Right: The Rue Saint-Pierre leads to the basilica's west front, whose tympanum was carved in 1856 during the church's restoration.

Facing page: The scallop shell of St. James, symbolizing the pilgrimage to Santiago de Compostela.

It's impossible to discuss Vézelay without mentioning its basilica. Yet its charming lanes, ancient houses, and the cuisine of chef Marc Meneau deserve attention too.

You can ask Marc Meneau—the prizewinning chef of L'Espérance, a superb hotel and restaurant where singer-songwriter Serge Gainsbourg spent the last years of his life (without ever crossing the threshold of the basilica)—anything you wish about Vézelay. His enthusiasm warms the heart. No one knows this place better than he does. "The five-hundred-year-old roots and soil of my village have taught me how to cook in a way that resembles me: it's a local cuisine, inspired by Vézelay. My father's saddlery, and my mother's café and grocery store, dictated a style of cooking that's like me. It's one that makes the eyes shine with pleasure, a combination of local influences, of my travels around the world, and of the development of tastes. Between 1970 and today, extensive building works converted the grocery store into an inn, and then into a 'Relais & Châteaux' hotel-restaurant where the kitchen gives us hope," explains the chef of L'Espérance. Keen to offer all-natural produce, he has his own vineyard and organic kitchen garden. Is he Vézelay's "mascot," as some claim? He doesn't seem to object to the suggestion.

Every wall, every street in Vézelay drips with history—some of it significant, some of it less so. It was here in 1146 that St. Bernard of Clairvaux preached the Second Crusade in the presence of Louis VII and Eleanor of Aquitaine; and it was here in 1190 that Philip Augustus and Richard the Lionheart met before joining the Third. At a bend in a lane one comes across the Porte Neuve abutting a twelfth-century wall. This "new" gate is famous for its appearance in the Resistance comedy *La Grande Vadrouille* (*Don't Look Now . . . We're Being Shot At!*), in which actors André Bourvil and Louis de Funès speed through it on their bicycles. Indeed, the majority of the night scenes, such as the one in which the two stars hide from the Germans, were filmed here.

At Le Pontot, the café at the foot of the basilica where the villagers usually meet up, Marc Meneau pops in for a drink. "Those who come to Vézelay looking for Jesus should realize that he's in this house," he booms, giving the proprietor's hand a goodly shake. "Hi there, Jesus, I've come to have a look at your pretty house. Jesus dwells in this seventeenth-century house and he also lets out rooms. Who'd have thought it? You can even sleep with the angels!" Everyone nods, laughing. But if there is one place Marc Meneau adores, venerates even, more than any other, it is the basilica's gardens. Standing squarely in front of the vast horizon, he exclaims: "It's really beautiful. I'd so love to be a painter; green, blue, yellow—the colors!"

# BRITTANY

Saint-Suliac
Locronan

BORDERED BY THE OCEAN from Brest to Rennes, and from Saint-Malo to Vannes at the westernmost tip of France, Brittany is a country of the sea: Armor—a land of ports, beaches, and cliffs. But it is also the land of Argoat, an expanse of woods, groves, and moors, home to granite villages. From afar, it seems like a wild place; but it is not immune to influences from outside, and it has its more convivial side. Though attached to its traditions, it is also a hive of innovation. Local headdresses and costumes, carefully conserved, are now worn only for special religious ceremonies and traditional festivals. Celtic to the bone, Brittany, with its feet firmly planted in moorland, is a place that believes in its dreams, a fact proven both by its historic achievements—castles such as Combourg, where Chateaubriand grew up, its gray silhouette flanked by four towers—and by the new technologies that flourish here. Robert Surcouf, Jacques Cartier, and all the fishermen who sailed to Newfoundland long ago show how adventurous and pioneering these Bretons are. The adventurous spirit continued in industry, with Fulgence Bienvenüe creating the Parisian subway, and, on a more human scale, with Vincent Bolloré and François Pinault giving a whole new dimension to time-honored materials such as paper and wood. In the wake of Brittany's brave seamen and yachtsmen like Tabarly and Kersauzon, sailing techniques and equipment have been improved by an armada of navigators. Fishing, shellfish farming, agribusiness, the production of specialties like the *kouign amann* of Douarnenez—all these enterprises energize the cities of Rennes (the regional capital and further education hub), Quimper, Lannion, Dinan, and Fougères.

Recently, music, ever a mainstay of the cultural landscape, has developed and diversified considerably. Following in the footsteps of the Celtic musician Alan Stivell, new singers have emerged. Year after year, Saint-Malo, Rennes, Lorient, Quimper, and Carhaix-Plouguer open their doors to the region's many music festivals.

*Facing page*: The coast at Ploumanac'h, one of Armor's more surprising sites. A lighthouse warns passing ships of the existence of large granite boulders. Pink in color, they have been worn smooth by the waves.

*Left*: In Loctudy, two Bigoudène ladies sport the traditional local headdress; the ocher sails of some *sinagots*, the pretty launches that ply the Gulf of Morbihan; two ancient megaliths at Camaret-sur-Mer on the Crozon peninsula.

# LOCRONAN

To the south of Finistère, three miles (5 km) inland, the village of Locronan sits at the foot of its sacred hill, the "Montagne" of the Druids who, it is believed, used to perform their rites here. The village coils around its Grand Place, ringed by fourteen strikingly beautiful large houses whose granite frontages date between the Renaissance and the eighteenth century.

Author Pierre-Jakez Hélias, who knew Brittany like the back of his hand, described this place as a "granite trough," dispensing food for the soul. Paved streets bordered by fine houses lead the visitor to the main square and on to the church of Saint-Ronan, built in the purest Gothic style. Almost unique, it has undergone no addition, modification, or restoration. It has come down the centuries intact, with its nave gently sloping up to the chancel, its altarpiece, its fifteenth-century stained glass, and a pulpit decorated with ten polychrome medallions recording the life of its patron saint—an Irish monk who arrived in Brittany in the seventh century and whose tomb is in the Penity Chapel next door. Anne of Brittany, wife of Louis XII of France, is supposed to have come here on a pilgrimage in 1505, begging the saint to grant her a male heir. Although her plea remained unanswered, she nonetheless elevated Locronan to the rank of town, an act that brought with it substantial financial advantages for its denizens.

Early on, the Locronanais, receptive to the beauty of their surroundings, were determined to try to protect it. Since 1924, they have seen it recognized as a "town of character" and voted one of the "Most Beautiful Villages of France." It has also long attracted interest from painters and filmmakers. In 1921, Henri Diamant-Berger shot *The Three Musketeers* here. Pierre Schoendoerffer used it as a backdrop for *Iceland Fisherman* in 1959,

HERVÉ LE BIHAN, a native of the village, is one of the last weavers in Locronan. Since childhood, he has taken an interest in local history and has given a new lease of life to his weaving workshop.

*Above*: Locronan curls around a
cobbled square, where sixteenth-
century manor houses in granite
are topped with steeply pitched roofs.
For a long time the well in the center
of the square was the village's only
source of fresh water.

*Left*: Hervé Le Bihan's workshop,
where flax and hemp—for centuries
the raw materials used for making
sailcloth—are still woven.

A uniquely harmonious architectural
ensemble, and very well preserved.
All in all, a glorious image of Brittany.

and Roman Polanski made *Tess* here in 1979. It was he who managed to get all the electric cables buried underground in the listed part of the village, making it still more harmonious. In 2004, Jean-Pierre Jeunet's *A Very Long Engagement* was filmed in the town, and France 3 chose it as the backdrop for a television series broadcast in 2011.

This town, whose heritage is still very much alive, owes its prosperity and much of its fame to the sails manufactured in its weaving workshops. Hemp has been grown all over the area since the fourteenth century. This crop spawned the production of sail-cloth, which benefited from the proximity of Pouldavid, the former port of Douarnenez. Of first-rate quality, it equipped the ships of the French Royal Navy and the French East India Company, as well as foreign fleets. The Spanish Armada may well have set course for England hoisting sails made of Locronan canvas. Motorization and mechanization put paid to the industry, but it is commemorated in the tools on display at the Musée d'Art et d'Histoire. Hervé Le Bihan, a man with the village in his blood, still practices this centuries-old but

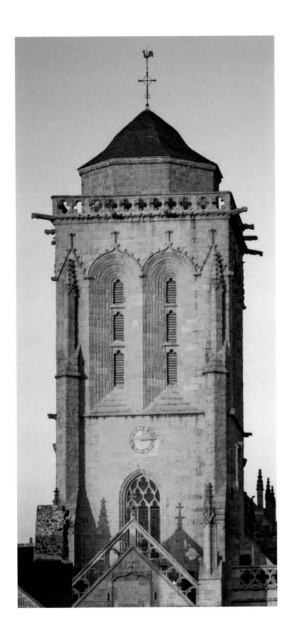

almost vanished craft, adapting it to the present day. In his workshop that doubles up as a storeroom, one can watch him at work, weaving hemp and flax into fabric for cushions, place mats, tablecloths, sheets, and bags. "Weaving is part and parcel of the village's history. When I set up the workshop, a hundred Locronanais, many of them elderly, came to see, telling me how delighted they were about the initiative. For them, the heart of the village had started beating again. They were so used to the sound of the shuttle being thrown and striking the frame at each pass, like a heartbeat," he tells us.

Hervé and his friends always participate in the Grande Troménie, a seven-mile (12-km) costumed procession around the village that takes place every six years, between the second and third Sunday in July. Accompanied by drums and bearing fluttering banners, the village inhabitants "beat the bounds" (in Breton, *tro minihi*), just as St. Ronan used to do around his hermitage. Every year when there is no Grande Troménie, a Petite Troménie, two-and-a-half miles (4 km) long, is held. To recuperate from their efforts, the participants, be they locals or tourists (Locronan welcomes some 450,000 visitors per year), are encouraged to continue the spirit of togetherness with a *kouign amann* cake or two, and to raise a glass to the future, to pleasure, and to good health in one of the bars that, along with the artisans' stores, line the village streets.

*Facing page*: Rue Saint-Maurice leads to the fine Gothic church of Saint-Ronan, whose surroundings form a glorious composition in grays and blues.

*Above, left*: The sturdy bell tower of Saint-Ronan, now shorn of its spire.

*Above, right*: The costumed procession of the Grande Troménie, a summer festival held once every six years.

# SAINT-SULIAC

With its steep streets and granite houses built around a port and a church, the village of Saint-Suliac, where the housefronts are still draped with fishing nets, has lost none of its identity or authenticity. Standing thirty-seven miles (60 km) from Rennes on the estuary of the Rance, and now listed and protected, it has refused to degenerate into a tourist trap, preferring to idle away the hours calmly. Once welcomed with a massive dose of sea air, newcomers are advised to don their sailing caps, because the inhabitants of Saint-Suliac have always known how to sail before even learning how to read or count. With its seven miles (12 km) of shoreline,

the commune is practically a peninsula. Breton to the bone, the pride and joy of the Côte d'Émeraude, and voted one of the "Most Beautiful Villages of France," it is wholly dedicated to sea and river.

At the summit of the town, the listed thirteenth-century church of the Ligueurs, one of the oldest in Brittany, gazes down on a maze of tiny, twisting alleyways from its strange fortified square tower. St. Suliac, a Welsh monk to whom all kinds of miracles are ascribed, lies entombed there, and sailors used to make offerings to the Virgin Mary to protect them from shipwreck. Wandering around the village's lanes that recall its long maritime history, the visitor might stumble across the chubby, cheeky-looking stone heads, sometimes

SERGE LELOUËT
With his bushy mustache
and gift of the gab, this retired
fisherman, whose son has
taken over at the tiller, runs a
secondhand store. He collects
and restores old maritime
objects before selling them
in his shop. Hopelessly in love
with the sea, he still likes
to take to the waters
in a traditional dory.

*Facing page*: The granite
housefronts along the sloping
streets of this little port on the
estuary of the Rance are adorned
with fishing nets, affording
a touch of authenticity.

*Left*: Dories are used for fishing
in the estuary, and flotillas of
them gather here in the summer
months.

*Top, left*: In the shade of a fisherman's cottage, a cat lies on a coil of rope watching the world go by.

*Top, right*: The thirteenth-century church of Saint-Suliac is one of Brittany's oldest. With its square fortified tower surmounted by an octagonal block, it presents an unusual silhouette.

*Bottom*: The ruins of a Viking encampment, located on public property by the shoreline. Only the stone foundations remain, which become visible at low tide.

*Facing page*: Statues of saints in the porch of Saint-Suliac.

*Take a trip on a chippe—a traditional craft used for fishing sand eel in the estuary.*

dating from the sixteenth century, that adorn the corners and façades of its old houses.

The stores at Saint-Suliac are full of goods—in particular the one belonging to antiques dealer Serge Lelouët. After thirty years spent chasing fish on the seven seas, and still with an almost obsessive passion for the ocean, he is delighted to serve as a guide. He has Saint-Suliac in his veins and knows every square inch. At the entrance to the "Rocher du Corsaire"—his very own Aladdin's cave, devoted to maritime memorabilia that he collects and, when need be, repairs—he explains: "One tree, three lengths of wood, and that makes you a boat—it's brilliant!" Boasting a great mustache and the gift of the gab, no one knows the history of this coastline where he used to drop anchor better than Serge. These days he continues to mess about aboard a dory, a traditional craft. "Long ago, nets were made out of cotton and were hung up to dry on the walls; people still do it now, but mostly for decoration," he remarks, before recalling how generations of sailors from Suliac would cast off for Newfoundland to fish for cod, many never to return.

An inveterate walker, Serge knows every path on the coastal trail that starts at Saint-Suliac and connects many interesting sites. Leading to the Beauchet tidal mill, which uses water power to grind the grain, it continues on to the old saltworks of Les Guettes, founded in 1736, their ten draining tanks protected by a dyke, and as far as Le Puits and the headland of Grainfollet. In 1894, an oratory dedicated to the Virgin, their patron saint, was erected there by the cod-fishers to thank her for having brought them home safe and sound from Newfoundland. The trail also takes in Mont Garrot, with its glorious views over the Rance estuary and elsewhere. Nestling amid apple trees stands a spectacular Neolithic menhir in white quartz stone, some sixteen feet (5 m) high, proof that the region was inhabited in prehistoric times. Ramblers' footpaths also give access to the countryside around Saint-Malo, Dol-de-Bretagne and Dinan, as well as Mont-Saint-Michel. If, though, you fall for Saint-Suliac's relaxed atmosphere, gardens, flower-bedecked housefronts, comfortable guesthouses, and the tasty cooking on offer in one of its grill rooms (such as the unmissable farm at Le Boucanier), or are captivated by its nine hundred chatty inhabitants, you can always shelter from the wind and idle away your day in the town. In that case, you can investigate that rarest of things, a Viking encampment. Located in a maritime zone open to the public, this enigmatic settlement takes the form of stone foundations that emerge at low tide. Those plundering men of the sea must have used it as a stronghold. Occupied probably between 900 and 950, it must have consisted of wooden fortifications to keep the Rance at bay, a projecting earthwork surrounded by heaps of stones, and an external entrenchment, surely stuck with stakes, to protect the longships on the landward side. Full of tall tales that fire the imagination, the entire village exudes the scents of childhood and of grandma's homemade jam.

# CENTRE

FROM THE BERRY REGION to the provinces of the Orléanais and the Perche, and from the Touraine to Sologne, the region of the Centre has long borne the royal hallmark. Picturesque, majestic, sometimes unpredictable, always inimitable, the Loire winds through it from east to west. Flowing past châteaux, castles, towns, and vineyards, the river lends a unique light that has inspired countless artists, beginning with Leonardo da Vinci. Its course can be followed on foot, on horseback, by bike or by car. You can glide over it in a hot-air balloon or navigate it by rowboat, passing through Gien, Orléans, Beaugency, Blois, Amboise, and Tour. The Loire châteaux are usually thought of as starting at Chambord, which Alfred de Vigny calls "a dream made reality." Here, everything feels larger than life: its beauty and grandeur, its architecture and décor. But the châteaux of Gien, Sully, Cheverny, Blois, and Chenonceau, and so many others besides, both on the river and inland, are worth stopping for. This extensive, beautiful region also offers a vast number of walking trails through its forests and along its riverbanks. In the regional nature reserve of the Brenne, which is known for its many ponds, areas of water, woodland, moor, and meadow vie for space. Rare butterflies, dragonflies, fish, frogs, water- and woodland birds, coypus and other large mammals can all be observed there. In the Loir-et-Cher, near Saint-Aignan, the ZooParc de Beauval covers seventy-four acres (30 hectares) and is acknowledged as one of the fifteen finest zoos in the world, boasting 4,600 animals, including Yuan Zi and Huan Huan, a pair of pandas lent by China. The region of the Centre also contains some of the finest cathedrals in France (including Bourges, Chartres, Orléans, and Tours), as well as the famous abbeys of Saint-Benoît and Noirlac, and, at Germigny-des-Prés, one of the oldest churches in the country, a rare example of Carolingian architecture.

*Facing page*: Way out in the countryside, Chambord—the largest and most prestigious château of the French Renaissance, and the brainchild of Francis I—stands at the gateway to the Loire valley.

*Left*: A stained-glass window representing the Apocalypse in the cathedral of Bourges (Cher); the box hedges in the ornamental garden of the château at Villandry (Indre-et-Loire) have been shaped into hearts, scrolls, and even musical notation; with its thousand ponds, the nature reserve of the Brenne is home to a rich diversity of fauna and flora.

# APREMONT-SUR-ALLIER

If you want to know what a village *in* a garden looks like, you should go to Apremont-sur-Allier, nine miles (15 km) from Nevers. On the banks of the Allier and dominated by its imposing castle, this village of just eighty-seven souls will appeal to lovers of nature and silence. With their shutters painted dark red, the village's houses are built in the typical medieval style of the Berry. There are no eyesores: no electric wires, no telegraph poles, no flashing neon signs. At night, the village is illuminated by wrought-iron lanterns. All is bathed in an ocean of blooms—especially the local park, which overflows into the village's only street.

This park, accorded the status of "Remarkable Garden" by the French Ministry of Culture, was planted at the beginning of the 1970s by Gilles de Brissac and is surely one of the finest contemporary examples of its kind. Damming off the valley with 600 tons of rock, this talented landscape designer totally reorganized the site, collecting water from the surrounding hills

and creating a waterfall. Wisteria, roses, and clematis thrive here beneath a pergola almost 330 feet (100 m) long, alongside rare specimens of conifers, evergreens, and flowering and deciduous trees. The park is dotted with viewpoints. Reminiscent of eighteenth-century *fabriques* (picturesque follies), these constructions are the work of Russian painter-architect Alexandre Serebriakoff. A dazzling red Chinese-style bridge, its pagoda roofed with fish-scale slates, spans a gentle brook.

*Left*: In Apremont—which has just eighty-seven inhabitants—a row of houses in the medieval style typical of the Berry lines the bank of the River Allier.

*Above*: At the château, a bright-red pagoda bridge, created in 1985 by the Russian painter-architect Alexandre Serebriakoff, invites the visitor to explore the gardens.

> The park is such an integral part of this peaceful little town that we call it a 'garden village.'

Since the death of Gilles de Brissac, his sister, a talented writer and recipient of several literary awards, has taken over the château, flower garden, and houses of Apremont-sur-Allier. A colorful character, she now lives in a house in the château's kitchen garden and spends her days "tramping about" the property. All the while overseeing the upkeep of the woodland and garden, and the management of the brewery, she still finds time to devote herself to her real passion, writing. The Brissac family has made Apremont their home for three centuries: Elvire's roots are here, and she couldn't imagine ever leaving. She is known and liked by everyone in the village. "In the Middle Ages these houses were inhabited by boatmen. They transported freestone extracted from Apremont's many quarries down the Allier," she tells us, before pointing to the oldest: "That one belonged to the harbormaster." The houses around the old square are still occupied. Elvire walks up to an elderly lady: "This is Suzanne Orfèvre, the memory of the village. She's seen every little change in Apremont." "Some time ago, I saw a meadow transformed into a marvel!" Mme Orfèvre replies. This marvel is, of course, the park: a bucolic landscape enjoyed by countless visitors since it opened in 1976. Tony, the head gardener, who looks after it every day, appears: "You can't explain Apremont. It's just gorgeous, and we are privileged to live here year in, year out."

The inhabitants of Apremont-sur-Allier form one big family, which likes to meet up on the banks of the river for birthday parties, wedding receptions, and a successful garden festival, generally held at the end of May. As they saunter along the banks, they might suggest that the visitor rent a canoe to view their village from another angle. Looking down on her nearly 5,000 acres (2,000 hectares) of woodland, Elvire adds: "I've planted 400,000 trees in my lifetime, including 300,000 oaks. I'll never see them grow up!" Nostalgic, perhaps, but what a glorious legacy.

*Facing page, top*: At one time, men would hew stone out of the quarries at Apremont and ferry it down to the Loire valley by river. A few lovely houses with pink-ocher fronts testify to this bygone industry.

*Facing page, bottom*: The château's enchanting gardens feature a number of *fabriques*, or follies, built in an eighteenth-century style. The Turkish Pavilion, shown here, conjures up images of the Bosphorus and the splendor of the Ottoman Empire.

*Above and right*: Dominated by the bluish gray of the château's roofs, the village's flower garden was inspired by Sissinghurst, the English garden planted by the novelist Vita Sackville-West.

# LAVARDIN

I n the Loir-et-Cher, approximately twenty-seven miles (43 km) from Blois, Lavardin is a dream in stone set high above the valley of the Loir. Secure from the upheavals of history, the village nestles at the foot of an imposing fort whose ruins hang prettily from the chalky slope. To see this haven's sun-kissed housefronts, one first has to cross the River Loir. Spanning 184 feet (56 m), a Gothic bridge supported by eight arches points the way, inviting us to wander down picturesque, flowery lanes lined with tastefully restored medieval houses and on to the castle promontory. Already known in the eleventh century, and furnished with an early masonry keep, it testifies to fierce feudal battles. For more than a century, the suzerains of Lavardin and Montoire waged a merciless war for superiority, before being reconciled by the Hundred Years War against England, when they joined forces to defeat Richard the Lionheart and then Henry II. Things were very different in the early days of the seventeenth

*Right, top*: A fine sixteenth-century town house with mullioned windows.

*Right, bottom*: The entrance to a troglodyte dwelling, now modernized into a comfortable living space. There are 446 examples in Lavardin, for a population of just 226 people.

*Facing page*: The village is guarded by the imposing ruins of a fort. After repelling Richard the Lionheart, it handed itself over to Henry IV, who demolished it.

*Above, top*: Like a dream of stone, Lavardin hovers above the valley of the Loir.

*Above, bottom*: Even if the laundrywomen have deserted the washhouse, fishermen still cast their lines into the sparkling waters of the Loir.

*Right*: Christ in Majesty, one of the superb Romanesque frescos in the church of Saint-Genest. They were rediscovered last century under a layer of seventeenth-century whitewash.

> The villagers may guard their quality
> of life jealously, but they are more than happy
> to share it with you.

century. The king's subjects in the province refused to recognize Henry of Navarre (also, through his mother, Duke of Vendôme) as ruler of France, on the pretext that he had once been Protestant. Henry IV marched on Lavardin, seized it, and razed its defensive walls to the ground.

No one could imagine a better guide to the village than Hubert Bretheau, whom everyone just calls "Hubert," whose office, the onetime priory of Saint-Genest, served as the presbytery until 1949. He likes to look down on his fiefdom from the keep. Rising to 148 feet (45 m) above ground level, it's well worth the climb. "I adore this view over the Loir, the river that makes our valley such a pleasant place to live. Vines were once cultivated here, though they're long gone. Still, we've kept the habit of meeting up to share in the bounty of the land." People like to get together around a fishing rod or two on the banks. "Twenty minutes before sunrise, we're at our posts. Around 8.30 we grab a bite to eat, then it's back to fishing until midday. Time for another snack, no hurry, with one eye on the float, and by then I'd say the day's well underway.... There are some extraordinary adventures to be had in Lavardin!" remark Ernest and Jean-Michel, two cognoscenti of quiet days spent at the water's edge. Another source of "adventure" is the "poet's walk" along the course of the Loir, so named in tribute to Pierre de Ronsard. This Renaissance "prince of poets" was born in the Vendômois, at the château of La Possonnière, a stone's throw away. The trail carries on past a Gothic house that once belonged to Florent Tissard, Francis I's ostler and staller, who built it in the sixteenth century. The frontage is embellished by an elegant corbeled turret. There is nothing to prevent you casting an eye over the priory of Saint-Martin, where Paul Claudel spent some time in 1928 writing his *Conversations dans le Loir-et-Cher*, or looking in on Sylvain's workshop, an extraordinarily adroit craftsman who can spin glass.

Above all, you should not leave Lavardin without taking a closer look at its curious troglodyte dwellings. There are 446 examples for just 226 inhabitants. The majority were hewn out of the rock by the stonemasons who built the castle. The visitor reaches them down a *rotte* ("path" in the local patois) used by goats. "Though many people think we live here in squalor and clad in animal skins, we have water, electricity, the Internet, all modern conveniences," explains Monique, who lives in a cave and runs a famous restaurant whose specialty is *gigot à la ficelle*. "I bore a hole in the bone and thread a string through it. Then I hang the whole lot above the glowing embers. Each time I walk past, I give it a turn, just as cooks used to do in the Middle Ages. We do everything in our caverns. This is our kitchen," this first-rate cook observes. The leg of lamb takes two to three hours to cook—just enough time for a hand of *chouine*, the local card game, whose world championships takes place in Lavardin each year.

# CHAMPAGNE-ARDENNE

Saint-Amand-sur-Fion

Essoyes

TO THE EAST OF THE PARIS BASIN, the Champagne-Ardenne region covers four departments: the Ardennes, the Aube, the Marne, and the Haute-Marne. The valley of the Meuse, a frontier river, with dense forests full of game and haunted by legendary figures, offers interesting walks for both experienced and less intrepid hikers. Strongholds, such as Rocroi and Sedan, fortified churches, and museums dedicated to the battles of World War I attest to the tormented past of this buffer zone. Charleville-Mézières, where the poet Rimbaud grew up, is home to the École Nationale Supérieure des Arts de la Marionnette, which every three years organizes a world festival of puppetry. The perimeter of the great vineyard, Champagne's "golden triangle," is delimited by three grand cities: Reims, where the kings of France were crowned; Épernay, whose magical cellars were dug out of chalk pits; and Châlons-en-Champagne, which, straddling the banks of the Marne, is a place of simple pleasures and architectural delights.

Between Saint-Dizier and Troyes (the knitting capital of France) are the great lakes of Der-Chantecoq and of the Orient forest, teeming with fish, which were excavated to absorb the floodwaters of the Marne and the Seine. The regional nature reserve of the Forêt d'Orient is home to flocks of birds. A triangular area rich in freshwater springs is bounded by Arc-en-Barrois, where the three-story steam machine belonging to a disused sawmill is now a listed historic monument; Bourbonne-les-Bains, the only thermal spa in Champagne-Ardenne; and the south of Langres, a gently sloping plateau graced by four lakes. This area contains the town of Langres, with its ramparts; the château at Cirey-sur-Blaise, where Voltaire stayed; and Colombey-les-deux-Églises, where General de Gaulle is buried.

*Facing page*: From golden yellow to bright red, a vineyard in Champagne displays some glorious fall colors.

*Left*: The nature reserve of the Forêt d'Orient and its three lakes offer a breath of fresh air in the heart of the Aube; Reims Cathedral was where the kings of France were crowned; some roofs in Troyes are protected by *essentes*, or small wooden shingles.

*Above*: The timberwork of the old houses in Essoyes, typical of the Champagne region, is highly attractive.

*Facing page, top*: Impressionist painter Pierre-Auguste Renoir's wife was from Essoyes. He and his family spent their summers in this delightful village.

*Facing page, bottom*: The pathways that make up the "Chemins Renoir" are the best way to discover the village, the valley of the Ource, and the surrounding woodland.

# ESSOYES

The great Impressionist painter Pierre-Auguste Renoir was one of those to fall under the spell of Essoyes, the native village of both his wife, Aline, and his housekeeper and model, Gabrielle Renard. It could hardly have been otherwise. Lying to the south of Troyes, eleven miles (18 km) from Bar-sur-Seine, this village of little more than seven hundred inhabitants sits at the edge of the bucolic and plentiful Ource, a peaceful little tributary of the Seine. The site must have been attractive at an early date, as men started to build there in Celtic times. In the Middle Ages the river provided the power for several paper mills. This industry, the mainstay of the area's economy, petered out at the end of the eighteenth century, leaving behind some splendid freestone houses.

The village's architectural heritage owes much to the Hériot family. Charles-Auguste Hériot, cofounder of the now defunct Grands Magasins du Louvre department store (source of a colossal fortune) was born here. He appears under the name of Octave Mouret in Émile Zola's novel on the retail trade, *Au Bonheur des Dames*, as a typical entrepreneur of the period. On the death of M. Hériot, the business was successfully taken over by his brother, Zacharie Olympe, who showed his gratitude to Essoyes. Acquiring the château, he substantially enlarged it in the neoclassical style. The commune bought it in 1936, converting the left wing into a school and the right into the tax collector's offices. The church also benefited from generous gifts on the part of the family, including stained-glass windows and a now listed organ. Several Hériots repose in an impressive vault in the cemetery. "Our cemetery is a

veritable museum," observes Bernard Pharisien—cousin twice removed of Aline Renoir and a great-nephew of Gabrielle Renard—whose years of research have made him the best historian of Essoyes and its famous characters. He has written a number of books on the subject. In black hat and glasses, he uses his storytelling talents to delight the curious. In the cemetery he halts before Renoir's tomb, surmounted by a

bust of the painter wearing a cap. Renoir is buried with two of his sons, Pierre (1885–1952) and Jean, the film-maker (1894–1979), as well as the latter's second wife, Dido Freire, who died in the United States in 1990. In another tomb just behind lie Mme Renoir, the artist's mother, his son Claude (1901–1969), and his grandson, Claude junior, son of Pierre, who died in 1993. This tomb used to be crowned by bronze bust of Aline, which was taken down in July 2005 and has since vanished. A few feet from the tomb of Mme Renoir stands that of sculptor Louis Morel (1887–1975), a native of the region who assisted Renoir. The tombstone of the Pichon family (1914) is one of Morel's pieces. Topped with a seated female nude, it shocked the public at the time and continues to surprise passers-by.

The Renoirs did not die at Essoyes, but they repose here forever. Pierre-Auguste spent many summers here. Once he had bought a house, the village became one of his main sources of inspiration, and the narrow, winding streets, the river, and the gentle light appear in many of his canvases. The painter erected his easel

> Essoyes is forever associated with the painter Renoir. Just like him, visitors fall easily for its old, traditional houses and surrounding landscape of vineyards and forests.

BERNARD PHARISIEN, great-nephew of Renoir's favorite model, Gabrielle, knows the village and its characters better than anyone. An evocative storyteller who likes to research his distant forebears, he narrates the history of Essoyes to tourists while conducting guided walking tours.

at many spots in the village to capture a scene, such as the washerwomen he painted in 1888. At the rear of a garden, the studio where he would shut himself away to work on his paintings has been converted into a museum. Now village property, it is open to the public, as is the Espace des Renoir, which is similarly dedicated to the artist and his family.

A stroll through Essoyes shows how a village proud of its past and its famous denizens can also prove an agreeable place in the present day. Many young couples come here to set up home. There is also a guesthouse for people just passing through; it was once a pavilion, built in the nineteenth century to lodge guests on hunting parties, and has been thoroughly restored by the present owner. "I found it and took it into my head to make it come alive again," he exclaims, raising a welcoming glass. "To Essoyes, to Renoir, to Gabrielle!"

*Facing page*: The house where Gabrielle Renard, Renoir's preferred model, was born.

*Above*: In 1906, Renoir had a sunlit studio built at the bottom of the family's garden.

*Right*: Open all year round, the Espace des Renoir hosts a permanent exhibition as well as temporary shows.

# SAINT-AMAND-SUR-FION

Located seven miles (12 km) north of Vitry-le-François, Saint-Amand-sur-Fion takes life easy. Ensconced between two hills on the banks of the Fion, a minor tributary of the Marne, the village includes two hamlets, Coulvagny and La Cense-des-Prés. Since remote times, humans have been attracted to the site by the power provided by its waters. The name of the little river is surprising: it seems to be Carolingian in origin, even if its exact etymology remains obscure. From the very early Middle Ages, the Fion, possessing the priceless advantage of neither drying out nor bursting its banks, has run through the heart of a parcel of land belonging to the cathedral chapter at Châlons. There were water mills already in those times. In 1189, a mill owner decided to leave on a crusade, selling the property to the Order of Malta, which converted it into a lazaret run by the Knights Hospitallers of Jerusalem. Since then the mill has been known as the "Moulin de la Commanderie" or the "Moulin de l'Hôpité." For as long as people can remember, the inhabitants of Saint-Amand have harnessed the hydraulic power of the Fion. The village once benefited from six mills, two of which have been entirely renovated. If mill work proper has disappeared, the river is still enjoyed by villagers, hikers, and especially anglers on the lookout for trout. From the church bridge or the Mathieu bridge the visitor can make out a number of small wattle-and-daub

On the Rue du Pont-de-l'Église is this traditional studwork farm, where life was organized around the main courtyard. Several generations would have cohabited here.

*Above*: The capitals in the church of Saint-Amand are carved with scenes depicting village life. This example shows the vine and its pests.

*Facing page*: The church of Saint-Amand was constructed in the twelfth century in the Romanesque style, but it burned down in the thirteenth century following a storm and was rebuilt in the Gothic manner. Its porch is typical of the region.

This is one of the finest churches in France. Its Flamboyant Gothic choir has earned it the nickname 'the Wonder of Saint-Amand.'

constructions: washhouses, all now private property, throwbacks to a time when the washing machine did not exist and the valley echoed to the sound of beaters. This village of one thousand inhabitants has inherited many cob and timber-framed houses from earlier trades. The farms are arranged around an enclosed yard that recalls the layout of the Roman *oppidum*, reached through a double gate. Life was organized in and around these courtyards, which included several small lodgings, the majority of the buildings being cattle sheds, stables, and grain or fodder stores.

A true local and an enthusiast for this traditional lifestyle, Sylvain Lanfroy has transformed part of the family farm into a homestay and regales his paying guests with its history. The farms were once separated by passageways. Full of charm and mystery, these lanes offer easy access down to the Fion and along its bank. Saint-Amand possesses its very own "marvel," which people come from far and wide to admire: the astonishing church, built between 1138 and 1147 in the Romanesque style, that the Godins (the name given to the town's inhabitants) characterize as "indescribable, staggering for a village church." The entrance is via a galleried porch, beneath which parishioners gather before going in. "It resembles a stretch of cloister," they say. The church itself preserves Romanesque portions, in particular the vestiges of a tower that contains a spiral stair. Thirteenth-century additions to this earlier fabric include a nave and the chancel, its very high vaults in the purest Flamboyant Gothic style lit by beautiful stained glass.

Close by is a spring known as the "Fontaine de Saint-Amand." Legend has it that this is why the church was erected here. Farther on, at the foot of Mont Moyotte, the waters of the Fontaine au Thé aid digestion and are reputedly an excellent remedy against stomach pains. Ascending the slope to the summit of Mont Moyotte, the visitor has views over the village and the river valley, crisscrossed by trails that attract ramblers in large numbers. And everywhere, as far as the eye can see, there are vines.

*Facing page*: The chancel of Saint-Amand, which dates to the thirteenth century, is separated from the nave by a curved rood beam supporting an eighteenth-century crucifix.

*Right, top*: Monique Fuinel, the "living memory" of the village, in the main room of the half-timbered farm where she lives. It smells pleasantly of beeswax, elbow grease, and peaceful living.

*Right, bottom*: The church porch is not used just for parish gossip: the village cats like to hold secret meetings there, too.

# CORSICA

Corbara

Piana

DEAD-PAN HUMORISTS have observed of Corsica that it is "a land of mountains in the sea." Geographers, meanwhile, divide the island into two Corsicas: the east is a terrain of schist, which provides *lauze* roofing stone, while the western side is of granite, where the tile reigns supreme. Tourists who venture through these inapproachable, steep-sided valleys will encounter many "islands" within the island. Rising to 8,878 feet (2,706 m), Monte Cinto, the watchtower of the Balagne, represents the island's highest point and, like the Punta Minuta and other peaks on the range, offers a playground for lovers of mountaineering. Over six hundred miles of gorgeous coast act as a magnet to the less adventurous. To the east stretch long sandy beaches; to the west, the coast is rockier, indented, and conceals impressive gulfs where diving enthusiasts can explore the Mediterranean deep: here are the red of the Calanche de Plana and its creeks; the Golfe de Porto, which—according to local tradition—the devil hewed out of the land with an ax; the Scandola nature reserve, with its spectacular cliffs; and, farther south, Capo Rosso. All of these spots have been given World Heritage status by UNESCO.

Corsica is one island comprising eighty-nine islands and islets, the majority of which are mere rocks a few cable lengths from the shore. On land the plant life is resplendent, while grouper and coral thrive in the waters. Corsica is best explored on foot. Perched on its heights, and clinging to the sides of its hills, its villages—where communities still practice an age-old style of singing—share a notable architectural unity. In the guesthouses and restaurants, specialties include delicious charcuterie and astonishing cheeses, as well as eel and trout from fast-flowing streams.

*Facing page*: The pink-granite Capo Rosso, on Corsica's westernmost tip, rises to 1,086 feet (331 m) above sea level.

*Left*: The port at Ajaccio abounds in bright colors, dazzling light, and mouthwatering smells; with nearly six hundred miles of coastline, Corsica offers some rich and varied diving; Sartène—"the most Corsican of all Corsican cities," according to Prosper Mérimée—appears like an extension of the Monte Rosso.

# CORBARA

I n the Balagne, situated between the Île Rousse and Calvi, the houses of Corbara trundle down the side of Monte Guido to the sea. White-painted and capped with red roofs, Corbara displays a Mediterranean splendor that verges on the impudent. At its feet stretch four miles (7 km) of sandy coastline divided into six beaches, together with a very chic marina at Davia. The name of Davia is inextricably bound up with Corbara. The story runs that Davia was an exceptionally beautiful girl from the village who was celebrated across Corsica. Her real name was Marthe Franceschini, and she was the daughter of a poor fisherman but ended up in the harem of the sultan of Morocco, Mohammed III (1750–1790), rising to become Sultana Dhawiya, "the luminous." How on earth did that happen? The old legends tell us nothing about her real life, alas, and all we are left with is an enthralling fairytale. At any rate, her fabulous destiny is responsible for the Casa dei Turchi close to the town hall—the "House of the Turks," supposedly built on the orders of the beautiful sovereign for her brothers, who stayed behind.

"Why should we go anywhere else when we have everything here?" the thousand inhabitants of Corbara might well ask, pointing to the sun-kissed sky, the clear blue sea on the horizon, the mountains within reach, and the surrounding hills covered in prickly pear and olive and lemon trees. Market-gardener Pierre-Antoine Savelli recalls how at one time the Balagne was the garden of Corsica, with Corbara at its epicenter. But horticulture has far from disappeared. He is living

*Right, top*: Situated beneath the monastery of Saint-Dominique and built in 1765 is the chapel of Notre-Dame de Lazio, where services are held all year. Every August 15 the chapel celebrates a Mass of the Assumption followed by a procession.

*Right, bottom*: The fine-sand beaches of Bodri and Gjunchitu, about one mile from the Île Rousse, are lapped by limpid waters.

*Facing page*: Built around 1430 on the side of Monte Sant'Anghjulu, the monastery of Saint-Dominique is the largest in Corsica and now offers retreats.

Without any doubt, Corbara boasts some of the most significant and interesting pieces of ecclesiastical heritage in all of Corsica.

AMADEI NONCE, called "Nono," would never dream of leaving his village and enjoys his chats with the brothers of the Congregation of St. John at the monastery.

proof, since he still brings fruits and vegetables to be sold at the monastery of Saint-Dominique. Erected in about 1430 on the slopes of Monte Sant'Anghjulu, the abbey, now listed and the largest on the island, is occupied by brothers of the Congregation of St. John, together with its enclosed orchards and gardens. In addition to their agricultural activities, the monks converted part of the property into a retreat where visitors can stay for a day, a week, or longer. "The brothers do not provide rooms solely for Christians. Their door is open to all, to all those who search, to whom they try to bring a touch of joy, so that they can set out again reconciled with themselves and more open to others," explains the mayor, Paul Lions. The monks' cells have been converted into bedrooms; one early occupant was the author Guy de Maupassant, who stayed in 1880, while a century later Alain Peyrefitte, author and onetime minister under General de Gaulle, found this a calm spot for writing. Come evening time, the view from the top of the terrace down on Corbara, whose

various quarters are arranged like the tiers of a Roman amphitheater, is amazing.

Corbara boasts two castles, the first dating to the fourteenth century and demolished by the Genoans in the sixteenth, the second built on older, defensive remains. In 1710, a small chapel was installed in what used to be the weapons' hall. Of disarming simplicity, and containing one sole item of decoration—a *pietà* dominating the main altar—the chapel is dedicated to Our Lady of Sorrows. Down cobbled lanes and covered passageways, the visitor reaches the collegiate church of A Nunziata, a vast baroque barrel erected between 1640 and 1715 on the plan for the cathedral at Bastia— and not much smaller. Inside, the eye is drawn to the high altar, carved from Carrara marble, and the sculpted walnut pulpit. The Musée du Trésor next to the church features an impressive ensemble of 152 church vestments dating from different periods.

Based in his own house in the heart of the village, Guy Savelli's private museum also deserves more than a cursory glance. This Corsican with a passion for history has gathered together unusual objects that all in their way have something to say about his native land. Pictures, documents, coins, books, furniture, and musical instruments tell of occupations that still exist at Corbara, often using the same age-old skills: carpenters, potters, olive-growers, pork-butchers, cheesemakers, musicians.... With a laugh, the jolly fellow notes: "In Corbara, there's the chapel where you pray and two where you drink. But there are more people in those two chapels and a hell of an atmosphere. Somebody will always break out into a song and it's soon taken up by everyone else."

*Facing page*: Set amid Mediterranean maquis, olive trees, and holm oaks, with a view over the sea, Corbara is a pleasant town that grew up around its collegiate church of A Nunziata.

*Right, top*: Occupied by the Congregation of St. John of Jerusalem, the monastery of Saint-Dominique welcomes all types of visitor within its walls, believers or not.

*Right, bottom*: The Bar de la Place: one of two "chapels" in Corbara where the inhabitants like to meet up.

*Above*: Occupying a headland overlooking the Golfe de Porto and the Mediterranean, Piana provides a charming crash course in Corsican architecture.

*Right*: The Italian-style church of Sainte-Marie was built from 1765 and was paid for by public subscription.

*Facing page*: Corsican charcuterie: (from left to right) *coppa*, *figatellu*, *lonzu*, and dried sausage.

# PIANA

O n the island's west coast, north of Ajaccio, no more than one hour by car at most, Piana gazes down over the Mediterranean. Seated on a headland 1,476 feet (450 m) above sea level overhanging the Golfe de Porto, it offers a delightful digest of traditional Corsican architecture. Its stone-built houses laid out in terraced rings, its shady squares and fountains, its immaculate white Baroque church of Sainte-Marie and thrusting bell tower, and its cobbled lanes have earned it recognition as one of the "Most Beautiful Villages of France." For Michel Fugain, who fell in love with it more than twenty years back, it ranks as the "most beautiful village in the world." And its five hundred inhabitants would brook no contradiction. Anyone who has been to Piana once wants to return. Tourists admit it freely, and take back souvenirs made by local craftsmen just in case. These are often decorative objects made of driftwood found on the beach and smoothed by wind and sea. It's worth making a halt at Angelo's, Piana's accomplished pork butcher, who specializes in products from the Corsican wild pig. This animal feeds exclusively on what it forages from the forest floor: sweet chestnuts, acorns, and the roots of the maquis scent the meat. *Figatellu*, an excellent liver sausage best eaten raw, *coppa*, dried spine, and meatballs of dried cheek can be savored in situ or taken home in the luggage hold. Strongly recommended is the *brocciu*, which is served savory or sweet: a goat's- or ewe's-milk delight considered by the Corsicans as their "national" cheese and cured, as tradition demands, in the village by four families of shepherds.

At the end of the village, those in the know take a path that winds agreeably through the *machja* (maquis) to the Ficajola creek. It takes a mere ten minutes. Sheltered between towering rocks and protected from the wind, this beach of tiny pebbles opens onto a turquoise sea. In the middle of several *calanches* (a Corsican word meaning "creek"), it offers a superb view over the natural park of Scandola. Rain and wind have carved deep into the rock, resulting in some surprising shapes. Red scarps some 980 feet (300 m) high and as sharp as needles emerge from the pine forest and scrubland before plunging into the sea. One of these contains the "Lovers' Rock," which nature has formed into a heart. Legend records how the devil fell in love with a shepherdess, who refused his advances. To punish her and her mortal lover, the evil one imprisoned them above this heart. With a little imagination, the old fishermen say, you can just make out the form of two lovers, face to face.

The creeks appear no less beautiful from the sea or from one of the hotel terraces that hug the hillside.

In every season, the residents of Piana like to make their way down to the beach at Ficajola where the fishing vessels are moored. Visitors are sure to bump into Antoine Bacchidu, one of the two professional fishermen in the village. Antoine is at his busiest in April and May, and sells his fish to three restaurants that await them impatiently. Every day for forty years, Philippine, a cook deeply attached to her restaurant and to the surrounding landscape, has gazed at each catch for inspiration, turning it into a source of delight for her guests. Fifteen minutes in the oven and it's ready. Grilled lobster with a view over the creek; there are worse things in life. As the day advances, the boulders display a changing palette of hues, from red through orange to pink. In 1884, Guy de Maupassant observed this spectacle, spellbound: "The astonishing rocks took the form of trees, plants, animals, monuments, men, monks in their cowls, horned devils, enormous birds, a whole monstrous populace, a menagerie that some extravagant god had turned to stone," he wrote in *Une Vie*, after a stop in Piana.

At the *calanche* in Piana, you can have fun looking for animals, people, and symbols in these rocks shaped by nature.

*Facing page*: Ensconced between two cliffs, the tiny beach of Ficajola is sprinkled with fine, golden sand. Its turquoise waters are an open invitation to swim or laze about.

*Above*: The so-called "Lovers' Rock" in the creek in Piana. Nature has carved a heart through the rock, though legend maintains that it represents two lovers turned to stone.

*Left*: For forty years Philippine has worked in her restaurant, where the freshly fished lobster is a delicious specialty.

# FRANCHE-COMTÉ

A SYMPHONY OF FORMS and colors, this province at the border with Switzerland revels in some dazzling contrasts. From Vesoul to Lons-le-Saunier, nature seems to have fashioned the terrain with love. The result is some serene countryside, varied in landscape (the forests are particularly rich), where the fauna and flora are frequently protected.

In the Haute-Saône are oaks and beeches, in the Doubs, firs and spruces, and on the plains grow hornbeam, wild cherry, maple, and birch. Water flows from the Jura to the valleys of the Loue, from the basins of the Doubs and the Saône through the country around Dole and on to the Vosges, feeding several thermal spas. The region has some 3,400 miles (5,500 km) of river, including the Doubs, which, close to its source at Noirmont, percolates into cracks in the limestone to emerge as a lowland waterway running through the Bresse in the Châlonnais. The result is one thousand ponds, ninety-one lakes occupying valley floors like those at Saint-Point and Remoray, and countless waterfalls, streams, and brooks.

Geologically, the region is dominated by the Jura mountains. It is the part of France farthest from the sea, and offers a range of year-round leisure activities. In every village the inhabitants' way of life has been shaped by the local climate, harsh in the uplands and milder on the plain. Whether large or small, such towns as Dole, Vesoul, Belfort, Besançon, and Montbéliard have all restored and pedestrianized their historic centers. A zone of exchange in spite of the mountains, wedged between Alsace and Burgundy, and not far from the region around Lyon, the Franche-Comté region cultivates the art of fine living and good food, making the most of its excellent local produce. Without neglecting such classics as morel pie, trout or coq-au-vin accompanied with Arbois *vin jaune*, or Morteau sausage with Comté cheese, chefs now devise innovative dishes based on high-quality meat and Bresse poultry.

*Facing page*: Nestling at the heart of the Jura Massif, Crouset is a typical mountain village of the Franche-Comté.

*Left*: A woodpile waiting to be carried off; a waterfall at Hérisson in the Jura; Comté cheese maturing in the Fort Saint-Antoine, where each truckle is regularly cored and turned over.

# BAUME-LES-MESSIEURS

A single road between Champagnole and Lons-le-Saunier leads to Baume-les-Messieurs. Three green valleys, hemmed in and then blocked off by gleaming, vertiginous cliffs, meet at two "dead-ends" that in Franche-Comté are called *rec-ulées*. This extraordinary place is home to an ancient town and an abbey next door. The contrast between the awesome scenery and the modest village is breath-taking. Time has lent a gentle curve to its roofs, and its leaning stone walls seem grateful for the help of the Virginia creeper and the hollyhocks.

The houses huddled around the abbey have narrow gardens bordered by low drystone walls. More than a whiff of nostalgia hangs about this town, which seems to look back on its past with fondness. In 909, Abbot Bernon endowed it with an abbey whose fame shone throughout the Middle Ages. That year, according to tradition, on the orders of the duke of Aquitaine, this same abbot—who was determined to revise the Rule of St. Benedict—left with six monks to found the abbey of Cluny, the spiritual beacon of the West. When the property of the Church was sold off during the French Revolution, the villagers bought the abbey church,

*Facing page*: Set deep within its valley—an impressive cutting in the chalk plateau of Lons-le-Saunier—the Benedictine abbey of Saint-Pierre has watched over the village of Baume-les-Messieurs since the ninth century.

*Above, left*: The Romanesque architecture of the abbey church of Saint-Pierre is strikingly austere. The aisles preserve their original vaulting.

*Above, right*: A celebrated sixteenth-century Flemish triptych, presented to the abbey by the city of Ghent in 1525.

which later served the needs of the parish. Since the nobles of the region enjoyed the privilege of being interred beneath its pavement, the nave preserves around forty old tombs. The abbey, the proud possessor of a sixteenth-century Flemish triptych alight with gold leaf and of an intact abbot's residence, has converted four cells of a sixteenth-century building into comfortable guestrooms.

Today, Baume-les-Messieurs has a population of two hundred—people who either were born here and are still passionately in love with the place, or have come here for its quality of life. Marcel Vuillemey, eighty years young, a retired antiques dealer and a painter in his leisure hours, knows every nook and cranny of the village's history, with both a big and a small "h." He maintains that Édith Piaf's song *Les Trois Cloches* ("The Three Bells"), with its chorus "Une cloche sonne, sonne," was composed by Jean Villard after he got lost on his way back to Paris one day and encountered Baume. Here, as in the song, the village bells ring three times: first those of the little church, then the abbey, and finally the bell at Granges-sur-Baume. Not short of a word or two, Marcel observes with a twinkle how "people come to see the place and the abbey, then stop to watch us playing skittles," a typical game in the Jura.

I really enjoyed this authentic
little town at the heart of
a site of outstanding natural
beauty. Don't miss the
view over the village from
the Cirque de Baume.

In summer, the preferred means of transport for visiting the main valley is a horse-drawn carriage, though it can also be explored on a locally hired mountain bike. Almost a mile long, the beautifully shaded *reculée* known as the Cirque de Baume flows with waterfalls. Its splendors include the monumental Cascades des Tufs, whose silvery waters and rocks covered in bright green moss can be observed from a belvedere that also offers glorious views into the gully and, beyond, over the entire Jura. Lastly, the visitor should try to make a visit underground, taking a guided tour of the nearby caves (closed in winter owing to flood risk). They are reached via a footbridge and a Gothic-looking arched corridor almost 300 feet (90 m) long. Visitors are greeted by five chambers carved out of the rock long ago by water. This section of the cave network, some 30 million years old, was discovered in 1610. Only about one third is accessible to the public and provided with walkways. The vault 262 feet (80 m) above one's head ensures an excellent acoustic, and for a long time the Baumois used to hold hunting-horn concerts here on August 15 every year.

Following a visit to the caves, the visitor might choose to watch the waterfalls from the shade of a small late nineteenth-century house, now converted into a restaurant. The abbey also has a terrace restaurant, where you can sample a sandwich filled with trout flavored with "bear's garlic," a wild variety with which the beasts supposedly purge themselves when they come out of hibernation. Baume-les-Messieurs: it's that kind of place.

MARIE MEIGE, a young energetic woman born into a local family, feels a strong connection with nature. She has opened a store, known as La Chaudronnette, where she sells plants collected in the nearby forests. She also makes "Drôlipathes": amusing figurines assembled out of plant material and nettle-bast threads. There are stores run by other craftsmen in Baume, too: a glassmaker, a potter, and a jewelry designer, among others.

*Facing page*: A little river, the Dard, emerges from the caves and cascades down the tuff—a rock formed by layers of chalk sediment. Regarded as some of the most impressive in Europe, these falls are ideal for trout fishing.

*Above*: The history of this exceptional site is visible in its houses, the low dry-stone walls that enclose patches of land, and the small, carefully maintained gardens.

# PESMES

The stonework and river of Pesmes—a kind of gateway from the Franche-Comté to Burgundy—make it a delightful place. Officially classified as one of the "Most Beautiful Villages of France," the village is perched on a rock over the Ognon, a calm and peaceable branch of the Saône. Protected behind the remnants of its fortifications, the houses are arranged in bands from river to hilltop.

For Éric, a young theater director born and bred here, no words are too good for his commune. "On one side, you have nature, the broad and generous Franche-Comté. On the other, by just lifting your head you can see the legacy of centuries and centuries in stone," he exclaims, his face full of passion.

When was Pesmes founded? No one knows with any certainty. It was already a baronetcy in the tenth century, and was elevated to a march in 1754. A fortified town strategically located on the road from Gray to Dôle, it was taken and occupied on several occasions, but today is still standing. The now listed buildings testify to a prosperous past and a thriving economy. Walk up the Rue des Châteaux to see its splendid medieval houses, tastefully restored. "They have resisted fire and destruction," Éric enthuses, now accompanied by Julienne, a Pesmoise and a keen historian. The Maison Royale, a fortified residence dating to the fifteenth century, with a delightful interior, has been converted into a guesthouse. "The Hôtel Mouchet de Châteaurouillaud, an L-shaped great-house of the fifteenth and sixteenth centuries, was an integral part of the town's defenses,

*Facing page, left*:
A sixteenth-century Virgin and Child, carved from Poligny marble, adorns the retable in the Andelot Chapel of Pesme's parish church.

*Facing page, right*: The Rue du Donjon, a medieval street that leads to the inner town through a fortified gate.

*Above*: Perched on a rocky plateau over the River Ognon, Pesmes derives its charm from its mix of stone and flowing water, and from the marvelous harmony between built heritage and natural scenery.

A pretty medieval walled town with diverse
historic buildings, it provides a backdrop for a large
number of cultural and summertime activities.

particularly the Porte Loigerot," they explain. One of two survivors out of the six that once marshaled the guard, this gate defended the banks of the Ognon and provided access to the part of town around the opulently furnished twelfth-century church of Saint-Hilaire, which closes off the rear of the main square. "In the Middle Ages, the Ognon had to be crossed over a ford. New arrivals would request authorization to enter the village by way of the still extant hexagonal tower," our guides continue. It is through the second surviving gate, the Porte Saint-Hilaire, that every April the *cavalcade* enters town—a carnival procession complete with floats and music, clowns, and acrobats. It is a must-see event in the town's calendar, and everyone is expected to take part. "Pesmes draws in all villages from far and wide. This isn't just a heritage site, even if we are very attached to it and know how to keep it thriving and attractive. People, associations, and cultural activities also play a central role," insists Éric.

On the banks of the Ognon just outside the village stand a number of forging mills that for centuries were instrumental in bringing the town fame and fortune. Respected for their high-quality steel, they manufactured armaments and, once Franche-Comté was annexed to France, supplied cannon balls for the arsenal at Toulon. The seventeenth century saw efforts to rationalize production, accompanied by more aesthetic concerns. Making the most of its artificial island, created by a bend in the Ognon and a flood canal, the domain was enlarged by means of a vast garden, a park planted with trees, and an orchard. The ironmasters' great-house dominates the workshops and the workmen's cottages. The factory was decommissioned in 1992, and the estate has since become the property of the commune; its buildings, partially renovated, have been converted into a museum open to the public.

The favorite sport here is angling. The river teems with fish of every kind. "You start fishing very young with your parents, then your grandparents. It's a living tradition, a country, rural activity entirely in keeping with the village," a local angler informs us. After a cast or two, the budding fisherman can make his way to Robert's, the baker's, whose specialty is *tourte pesmoise*, a homemade pie of veal, pork, and chicken liver, marinated in white wine. It's wonderful food for a picnic at the foot of the ramparts or beside the Ognon, or after the two-hour walk to the viewing point over the valley, which reveals nothing but nature as far as the eye can see.

*Facing page*: At the foot of the upper town and its tall houses, these more modest dwellings represent the remains of the tanners' quarter. Cows have been grazing these green pastures for centuries.

*Left, top*: A carved gorgon's head from the Andelot Chapel in the church of Saint-Hilaire.

*Left, bottom*: This superb pulpit, sculpted in red and gray marble, in the church of Saint-Hilaire dates from the sixteenth century.

# HAUTE-NORMANDIE

Veules-les-Roses

Le Bec-Hellouin

ALTHOUGH IT HAS ITS ROOTS FIRMLY in the soil, bucolic Haute-Normandie also has one face turned toward the sea. Under changeable but forgiving skies that have inspired generations of painters, its forests, groves, and meadows scattered with apple trees stretch from the bends of the Seine to the snow-white limestone cliffs of Étretat. Castles, manors, dovecotes, abbeys, cathedrals, churches, and venerable cities—even industrial wastelands given a new lease of life—tell the story of a much coveted and much fought-over region. Monuments record the Romans and the Vikings, William the Conqueror and Joan of Arc, the D-Day landings.... Its capital, Rouen, is a splendid city. As Guy de Maupassant, a Norman writer if ever there was one, once wrote, it is "a vast town with blue roofs under a pointy-headed congregation of Gothic belfries... dominated by the cast-iron spire of the cathedral." In the seventeenth century, the region's ports, with Dieppe and Le Havre at their head, developed a flourishing worldwide trade, in particular with Louisiana and the French West Indies. Their resulting prosperity spawned some glorious châteaux, such as Taillis at Duclair and Bailleul in Angerville-Bailleul.

Following the arrival of the railroad system in Rouen in 1843 and in Le Havre in 1847, construction around the new stations mushroomed, sparking a local industrial revolution and fostering seaside tourism. Only 120 miles (200 km) or so from Paris, the shores around Caux, from where so many had left to fish for cod, became peppered with resorts. At the foot of towering chalk cliffs that plunge into the English Channel, the pebbly beaches of Étretat, Fécamp, Saint-Valéry-en-Caux, Dieppe, and Le Tréport soon became voguish destinations. And it is here that the produce of the Norman soil joins the glorious bounty of the sea in some celebrated recipes.

*Facing page*: The cliffs at Étretat, on the Côte d'Albâtre, are ceaselessly pounded by waves.

*Left*: The Maison Henri IV in Saint-Valéry-en-Caux, built in 1540; Haute-Normandie grows many varieties of apple; a trawler setting off from the port of Le Havre to fish for whiting, cod, and pollock.

# LE BEC-HELLOUIN

Betweeen Rouen and Lisieux in the Eure, Le Bec-Hellouin has resisted time. Nestling in a calm and peaceful valley, and surrounded by coppices and meadows, it is a charming village, its narrow, well-shaded streets lined with half-timbered houses decorated with window boxes. It owes the first half of its name to the word *bec*, which in Old Norman meant a brook, and the second to the Blessed Herluin, who founded the splendid abbey here in 1034. It quickly became a religious center and was much respected by William the Conqueror. In 1045, a school opened for the education of oblates and sons of the nobility, whether or not they had an ecclesiastical calling. If its fortunes were mixed during the Hundred Years War and the French Wars of Religion, the determination of its community has never wavered. Proof of this is provided by the Tour de Saint-Nicolas, which guarded the entrance to the village and kept its inhabitants safe. Of imposing dimensions, the tower was built in the fifteenth century and is a telling sign of a return to prosperity. Today it is 148 feet (45 m) high; it used to measure 197 feet (60 m) until a fire brought down the spire in 1810.

Christian Falce, whose family has lived in Le Bec for three centuries, adores this village of little more than four hundred souls. He chairs an association that once a year organizes a plant sale and a secondhand-goods market, together with stalls selling homemade local food. The event mobilizes the whole village, and friends and neighbors are roped in to serve at the snack bar. All are happy to lend a friendly hand. The assistant mayor puts on his cook's hat and flips pancakes. "We Bretons just have to stand firm," he says with a laugh, proud of this prime example of village vitality.

Christian especially enjoys telling the story of his birthplace. At the outset, these clapboard houses were erected for the workmen building the abbey. At the invitation of the abbot, Dom Paul-Emmanuel Clénet (a great privilege, since the staircase is normally out of bounds to the public), he climbs the two hundred steps of the Tour de Saint-Nicolas, so named because its façade features a statue of the saint, alongside seven others. At the very top of this last vestige of the abbey church (it did not survive the Revolution), he looks proudly at the five bells set up little more than two years ago, which give him a great sense of community ("That's the least I can say!").

Since the whole site was listed and then recovered by the Benedictine Order in 1948, the abbey has risen from the ashes and now goes from strength to strength. Composed today of a chapter house, a seventeenth-century cloister, and the church (which took the place of the old refectory), it houses a monastic community

*Facing page*: Characteristic half-timbered houses in the village of Le Bec-Hellouin.

*Left, top*: A fleur-de-lys blazoned in flint on the Tour de Saint-Nicolas.

*Left, bottom*: The parish church of Saint-André, which houses many statues removed from the abbey during the Revolution.

> This is a typical Norman village, with timber-framed houses, and calm, attractive streets. A haven of peace, it's also home to a community of Benedictine monks whose handmade ceramics are much sought after.

that alternates between manual and intellectual work, carried out in silence, and prayer. Today, it numbers fifteen Benedictine monks, who run a pottery workshop and whose products are sold both at the abbey and online. They have reassembled a library currently containing 90,000 volumes, including 5,000 on the subject of Anglicanism deposited by the archbishop of Canterbury—a see with which Le Bec has maintained a close relationship ever since the Middle Ages. Using a computerized catalog constantly updated with notes, as many as twenty-four researchers can consult these materials in a onetime storeroom now fitted out as a reading room. In accordance with Benedictine

tradition, the abbey provides retreats for visitors and groups, and also accommodates young people keen to share in the life of the community for longer periods.

Tourists can of course take rooms at the hotel or eat in the restaurants on the village squares that border the main street (the Rue Saint-Anselme, named for the second abbot, Herluin's successor in the eleventh century). A great scholar, Anselm attracted pupils from France, Gascony, Brittany, Flanders, Germany, and even Rome to Le Bec. With its wooden-sided houses, the place is terrifically picturesque. Those looking to spend their vacation here can rent the old mill close by.

*Top, left*: Except for the medieval gatehouse, the abbot's residence was rebuilt between 1732 and 1735. The abbey includes a chapterhouse and cloister.

*Top, right*: The abbey of Notre-Dame—a center of Benedictine power from the eleventh century—was returned to the monastic order in 1948, following centuries of occupancy by cavalry and armed forces, notably during the French Revolution and World War II.

*Facing page*: Flamboyant Gothic in style and 148 feet (45 m) high, the Tour de Saint-Nicolas stands at the foot of the brook (the *bec*) that gives the locality its name.

*Above*: A thatched cottage
with a row of irises growing
along the ridge of its roof.
The plants prevent the
straw from drying out
and crumbling.

*Right*: Boats are dragged
ashore by tractor.

*Facing page*: A flock
of lesser black-backed
seagulls fishing at dawn.

# VEULES-LES-ROSES

On the Côte d'Albâtre, one hour's drive from Rouen, Veules-les-Roses basks in the fresh air. A ravishing village, it also offers a brimming bowl of good cheer to go with it. One of the oldest settlements in the Pays de Caux, it is fortunate enough to combine the charm of the countryside with the charms of the sea. Harmonious houses built in brick, flint, and timber line a long beach of fine sand at low tide and of pebbles at high. The village is clustered around the Veules, the smallest principal river in France, which lent the place its name, turned its grain mills, and provided the water in which the inhabitants rinsed their wool. Nestling since the fourth century in the hollow of a valley fanning out to sea, it long served as a fishing port from which dories would sail out to set nets, traps, and lines. At low tide, the villagers would fish for shrimp and sand eel. In the eighteenth century they also worked as weavers, making cotton fabric for Rouen.

Since the mid-nineteenth century, Veules-les-Roses has transformed itself into a busy resort. The cause of the metamorphosis was apparently a lady called Anaïs Aubert, an actress at the Comédie-Française, who, while unhappy in love, stumbled across this haven of peace. Taking along another famous actor of the time, Étienne Mélingue, they together launched the seaside career of Veules-les-Roses. Since then, countless celebrities (and unknowns) have come to hear the water sing in the millwheels, to choose their lunch from the morning's catch, to relax on the beach, and to enjoy the panorama from the cliff tops. Past visitors have included poet José-Maria de Heredia, Alexandre Dumas *fils*, the Goncourt brothers, and 1920s tennis champion Suzanne Lenglen. Even Victor Hugo stayed here with a friend, the playwright Paul Meurice, who had built a villa facing the sea. One Sunday, on September 24, 1882, the great writer threw a banquet for the hundred poorest children in the villages. That evening, fireworks were let

off from the cliffs. Painters, too—including the Russians Ilya Repin, Vasily Polenov, and Alexei Bogoliubov—have been bewitched by the light of the Normandy sky. Veules is still highly popular with artists.

Michel Robakowski succumbed so completely to the charms of this little town that he set up home here and now knows it like the back of his hand: "Welcome to the 'Champs-Élysées,'" he says with a chuckle on the square where the weekly market is held. "Because Veules does have its own Champs-Élysées. Well before the nineteenth century, there were fields here, and those fields belonged to one M. Élysées, hence

'Champs-Élysées.'" An expert on the village, he offers us the grand tour. "Here, we have the trough that at one time served as a ford, right in front of a typical thatched-roof cottage covered with plants to keep it damp and trim," he explains. The past comes alive in the village's architecture: cottages, grand early twentieth-century beachfront villas, and ship-shape fishermen's dwellings; and everywhere gardens of all sizes are overflowing with flowers—especially roses, hence the village's name.

Patrick, who grows watercress in the fast-running, chilly waters of the Veules, is a representative of an activity that began here in fifteenth century and is still very much alive. Excellent in soups, watercress is cultivated in Veules in the traditional manner. Fresh as can be and crunchy under the tooth, this crop comes in bunches that weigh a hefty twelve ounces (350 grams). Another glorious local ingredient, Veules's mud oysters—the only ones of their type in the Seine-Maritime—had vanished for period. But now these *Veulaises*, grown half a mile out to sea, are back and much in demand among gourmets. "Everything here is just wonderful," cries Michel from the cliff top: "The sky, the sea, the meeting of the two, all the greenery, the sky, and the water!"

Veules is extremely charming. This small village between sea and open country is a great place to stroll along the river past the watercress ponds or to admire the superb views of the cliffs on the 'Alabaster Coast.'

*Facing page, left*: A watermill wheel on the Veules—the shortest river in France, at just 1,300 yards (1,190 m) long.

*Facing page, right*: A grocer's store with blooming window boxes on the village square.

*Above*: The village is crossed by the Veules, in which wool used to be washed and whose lively waters support the growing of watercress.

# ÎLE-DE-FRANCE

IT IS UNDENIABLY STRANGE that an area with no coastline should be known as the "Island of France." Some say that the name comes from the fact that it's a spit of land enclosed by the Marne, the Oise, and the Seine; others see a corruption of *liddle Franke*, the Frankish for "little France." Only the old king Clovis could truly enlighten us, and he's long been dead. In any event, at the beginning of the Secondary period the Paris Basin formed a gulf surrounded by the massifs of the Ardennes, the Vosges, and the Morvan, and Brittany. Then the sea withdrew, leaving a sediment that now comprises the local soil. It was at this point that the three major rivers, as well as others of lesser importance, started to flow. Thus the area surrounding Paris is a harmonious balance between wide, fertile plateaus (Beauce, Brie, the Plain of France, and the Valois region), broad, green valleys, and the odd wooded hill. The nation's political, administrative, and economic hub, the Île-de-France is the very heartland of France and a historic crucible. Since the dawn of time, it has been a crossroads, but also a place where people settle, live, trade, learn, play sports, and enjoy themselves. Paris, with her monuments, museums, gardens, and performing arts, has tended to overshadow nearby satellite towns that nonetheless possess some impressive assets: which of Versailles, Fontainebleau, Chantilly, and Vaux-le-Vicomte is the most magnificent? Saint-Denis captures the imagination of every Frenchman, with its royal basilica and its stadium. The Chevreuse valley is alive with memories of the Impressionists and is now a place of further study. From its terraces, Saint-Germain-en-Laye, with its châteaux, museums, and gardens, looks down on the Seine. Throughout Île-de-France, and up to the very gates of the capital, numerous woods attract nature lovers.

*Facing page*: A view of Paris, at the heart of the Île-de-France, glimpsed through a clock face at the Musée d'Orsay.

*Left*: In fall, the forest of Fontainebleau shimmers with golds and reds; wheat ready for harvest in the Brie; the Marble Court at Versailles, the official residence of the kings of France from the time of Louis XIV to the Revolution.

# LA ROCHE-GUYON

One hour from Paris, on the road between Vétheuil and Giverny, La Roche-Guyon settles into a bend on the right bank of the meandering Seine. The finest view of this borough of 450 souls, nestling at the foot of the steep, protective wall of a plateau, is from the road along the peaks. In the heart of the Vexin nature reserve, of which it was a founder member, it remains the only village in the Île-de-France to have been selected as one of the "Most Beautiful Villages of France."

The keep of the castle for which the village is famous looks down on more than one thousand years of history. Its imposing silhouette has stood over this valley of chalk cliffs by the Seine since the Middle Ages. The old fortress has undergone many alterations over the centuries and is now an elegant miscellany of architectural styles. From the medieval keep to the eighteenth-century stables, from the great staircase and courtyard to the twelve-acre (5-hectare) "experimental kitchen garden" of the Enlightenment (guaranteed pesticide-free and open to the public since 2004), and from the ceremonial halls (some rehung with original tapestries) to the casemates fitted out by Rommel, visitors embark on a strange and enthralling journey through time. François de La Rochefoucauld, who owned the castle (it is still family property), wrote part of his coruscating *Maxims* here; Victor Hugo and Lamartine both stayed.

*Above*: At the foot of a chalk cliff in a bend of the Seine, streets of splendid half-timbered houses lead down to the château of La Roche-Guyon, fronted by a garden *à la française*.

*Facing page, top*: Proudly overlooking the Seine valley, the castle keep, supposedly impregnable, was built following the Treaty of Saint-Clair-sur-Epte in 911. It was designed to protect the border between the French and Norman territories.

It's best to explore the village from the Route des Crêtes, which overlooks the town. From here, you have a splendid view of the keep, the castle, and the banks of the Seine.

In a mysterious passageway hewn out of the rock, 250 steps connect the village's château to the old keep, which offers an awe-inspiring view.

The full-time guide, Martial Codina-Deslin, explains the castle's history: "The keep dates from the tenth century. It was built after the Treaty of Saint-Clair-sur-Epte in 911, which delimited the lands the king of France was to grant to the duke of Normandy. Protecting the border, the castle was considered to be impregnable. The rest was constructed between the thirteenth and eighteenth centuries. To the left of a courtyard where regular events (a garden festival, in particular) are held are some old stables reminiscent of those at Chantilly, with their large pediment bearing the sculpture of a bucking horse." Our guide then invites us to venture down a narrow tunnel hewn into the rock, and to take the 250 steps up to the impressive keep. "Up we go. It's pretty tough. You have to earn the view up here, but it's worth the climb," he puffs. From a height of 360 feet (110 m), the visitor gazes over the natural beauty of the Vexin, with its meadows and its cereal fields, and the village below.

On the bank of the gently flowing Seine, La Roche-Guyon's half-timbered houses line up as if on military parade. At the end of the cobbled streets one can catch sight of a number of cavities dug out of the cliff face. These are disused *boves*, where saltpeter deposits were excavated; they doubled up as byres and were employed until the end of the nineteenth century. Relatively constant in temperature, today these cavities are often converted into troglodyte dwellings. Back on the main square, the former exchange, which once stood on about thirty stone pillars, is now the town hall and market. Designed by Villars and decorated by the sculptor Jamay, the fountain was inaugurated in 1742 by Alexandre de La Rochefoucauld and supplies the watertower. The village's fifteenth-century church, dedicated to St. Samson—most of it erected during the English occupation during the Hundred Years War—features a marble statue of François de Silly, owner of the castle in the eighteenth century.

Before the railroad put paid to its ancient role, La Roche-Guyon had been a port catering for the stone quarries and the rolling-mills of Bray-et-Lû. Slopes that were once covered in vines are now wasteland; the last grape harvest took place in 1950. The village's long slumber, off the beaten track and far from the railway, has helped preserve its charm. Edgar P. Jacobs, author of the Blake and Mortimer comic books, set one of his stories, *The Time Trap*, here.

OLIVIA DESTAILLEURS, a potter, has set up her store in an old *bove*, or saltpeter cave. It was her great-grandfather who first took up residence in La Roche-Guyon, so as to be near his friend, the painter Monet. Practically the entire family followed, and they now have a house in the village. (In fact, Olivia's street is known as "Destailleurs's Rise.") Once the weather begins to improve, Olivia opens her workshop and gives lessons to local people of all ages. Her studio has become one of the busiest places in the village.

*Facing page*: The château of La Rochefoucauld was built gradually between the twelfth and eighteenth centuries. The court, bordered on the left by the old stables, often hosts events, including a large-scale annual garden festival.

*Above, top*: In the village, the sloping Charrière des Bois was originally intended to be just broad enough to allow a cart to pass.

*Above, bottom*: The château's stables were designed in the eighteenth century by the architect Louis Devillars. The main pediment features a lively sculpture of a bucking horse.

*Right*: An aerial view from the keep shows how the village clusters around the church of Saint-Samson, with its square bell tower.

The story of the village of Maincy
is closely linked to the château of
Vaux-le-Vicomte.

# MAINCY

The history of Maincy is intertwined with that of the great château of Vaux-le-Vicomte that lies within the commune's confines. Although it's close to Melun and has a good rail link into Paris, the village still has a country feel. In the midst of colza, wheat, and beet fields, surrounded by market gardens, Maincy's tranquil atmosphere has always attracted families with children, and its population is now more than 1,700. In Gallo-Roman times, it was the site of an opulent villa belonging to a certain Maincius, whose name, over time, became Maincy. Pavements, mosaics, heating conduits, and ceramics from the Roman era have been discovered around the church and close to the spring that supplied water to the settlement. It was on the site of this villa that the manor farm was later established.

Maincy forms a ring around a church fortified with a tower in the twelfth century—the period when locals began to extract stone and manufacture lime here. Life in the village carried on as normal until the seventeenth century, when Nicolas Fouquet arrived and changed everything. In 1656, the finance minister ordained the construction of a large château adorned with a vast ornamental park. The château was habitable just three years later. In the meantime, André Le Nôtre was busy designing the grounds. The celebrations held at Vaux on August 17, 1661, brought the building activity to an end. Maincy still possesses the housing scheme from the era, in which low terraces provided accommodation for the château's workmen or employees, grouped together by family or trade association.

"From that period, the château and the village have been interdependent. Formerly, all the inhabitants could enter the estate to collect wood or pick lily of the valley. They, too, were part of the history of the château, as neighbors, workers in the kitchen garden, or woodcutters in the park," Alexandre de Vogüé, owner

*Above, top:* The château's southern front opens onto a French-style garden of grand statues and neatly arranged avenues.

*Above, bottom:* When Nicolas Fouquet purchased the estate of Vaux-le-Vicomte, he commissioned the architect Louis Le Vau to enlarge the church of Saint-Étienne in Maincy, originally built under Philip Augustus. Le Vau's design incorporates a defensive tower topped by a belfry.

This rural village is known for the château of Vaux-le-Vicomte, but it also deserves to be explored in its own right. Enjoy a tranquil atmosphere that inspired the painter Cézanne.

of the estate, informs us, accompanied by an eighty-two-year-old villager named André, still with a spring in his step, for whom leaving the village is out of the question. Many farms have been newly restored and converted into homes, testifying to a venerable agricultural past. "I've seen herds of cows drinking at the trough on the square before returning to the cattle shed," André remarks, grabbing a stem of grass. "This is Maincy cress. At lunchtime people used to come and pay ten *sous* for a bunch of fresh cress that was picked right in front of them," he adds.

In compensation for the demolition of the old church of Saint-Laurent-de-Vaux, Louis Le Vau, the architect of the château, revamped the church of Saint-Étienne. The west front, with its majestic entrance door and covered porch, also dates back to this period. The fifteenth-century premises of the Carmelite Sisters to the rear of the Rue du Pavé-de-l'Église were purchased by the superintendent in 1658 and promptly restored; a tapestry manufactory directed by the court painter Charles Le Brun was established there, which ten years later transferred to Paris on the orders of Louis XIV, where it became the Manufacture des Gobelins. In addition to this original building, the village has a seventeenth-century almshouse founded by St. Vincent de Paul to house the poor, a press, an old watermill, and, on the main square, a long, rectangular washhouse of the nineteenth century, where washerwomen would do the château linen.

Immortalized by Cézanne, the bridge of the Trois-Moulins spans the Almont, a lively little brook. Mme Cofinet, a local with a passion for painting, is finishing a reproduction of this famous *Bridge at Maincy*, now in the Musée d'Orsay in Paris. The place has altered so little that we can tell at once that Cézanne's easel was exactly where we are standing. "It's patently a place worth preserving," she tells us. With its courtyards and gardens, its neat little houses roofed in tile, the rivulet that refreshes its charming lanes, and its beautiful château—a masterpiece of French Classicism that attracts visitors from all over the world—Maincy sees no reason to change. When the slates on the château's dome were recently replaced, a number of celebrities had fun sponsoring them: "Thierry Henry, Eva Longoria and Tony Parker, who were married here, Bill Clinton. I hope he still has that nineteenth-century slate on his mantelpiece," Alexandre giggles, prouder than ever of his village.

*Facing page, top*: The garden of Vaux-le-Vicomte is a perfect composition of *parterre de broderie* beds, statues, basins, grottoes, and vistas.

*Facing page, bottom*: The bridge of the Trois-Moulins spans the Almont. It was immortalized by Cézanne in a canvas entitled *The Bridge at Maincy*.

*Above*: Until washing machines became common, the washerwomen of Maincy would beat and rinse their linen in this long basin, built in 1853.

# LANGUEDOC-ROUSSILLON

Saint-Guilhem-le-Désert

Villefranche-de-Conflent

TANNED BY THE SUN, this region where the grapes still preserve the taste of wrath and the mountains a whiff of heresy is a dream come true for many vacationers during the great summer migrations. Stretching between the Rhône and the Pyrenees, from the fringes of the Lauragais to the Cevennes, its rolling plains and valleys sweep down to the sea like an amphitheater. The shoreline around the Golfe du Lion looks out to the Mediterranean, its chief inspiration. The five departments of Languedoc-Roussillon form a natural unit whose ties have been strengthened over the centuries by a shared history. Carcassonne, Narbonne, and Béziers know how to make common cause—even, when need be, looking west to Toulouse. Encamped on the northern slopes of the Pyrenees, Perpignan and French Catalonia are strongly marked by Spain. Nîmes is scented with all the fragrance of Provence. Mende, France's smallest prefecture—a veritable city in the countryside, sliced in two by the River Lot—hugs the Causse uplands, with the Massif Central rising not far off. Cutting-edge Montpellier, a university center that attracts students from far and wide, has assumed the mantle of regional capital with brio. The result is a singular amalgam of *boules* and cassoulet, bullfighting and Romanesque churches, bound together by two related languages, Occitan and Catalan. This was a Roman province before it asserted its independence from the princes of Toledo; it is associated with the creation and diffusion of Romanesque art, with the Cathar heresy, with Protestantism and the oppression of the Huguenots: every stone of Languedoc is rich with history. Unflinching, implacable, the sun drills into the landscape against a cloudless sky: hilltop villages, abandoned castles on arid peaks, and churches doze in the *garrigue*. The sun warms its sea, while trees around lakeshores and along rivers offer shade.

*Facing page*: Restored in the nineteenth century by Viollet-le-Duc, the walled city of Carcassonne, granted World Heritage status by UNESCO, testifies to a thousand years of military architecture.

*Left*: Ornamental ironwork on the door of Sainte-Marie de Mercadal, in the fortified medieval village of Castelnou; the wonderful light of Collioure beguiled Matisse, Derain, Picasso, and Dalí; the romantic ruins of Notre-Dame des Oubiels standing amid the vineyards at Portel-des-Corbières.

# SAINT-GUILHEM-LE-DÉSERT

In the gorges of the Hérault, on the frontier of the Massif Central twenty-two miles (35 km) north-west of Montpellier, Saint-Guilhem-le-Désert has been nestling in the middle of *garrigue*, gullies, and caves for more than ten centuries. Flanking the Val de Gellone formed by the Verdus, a tributary of the Hérault, this typically southern village huddles around its abbey. Scarcely altered and well preserved, it has kept its narrow lanes and masonry houses roofed with tile. Snuggling among the boulders and dominated by the Château du Géant ("Giant's Castle")—an imposing sentinel at the gateway to the "desert"—this medieval village has long been considered one of the most beautiful in France. To reach the village as the pilgrims used to do, you have to cross the Pont du Diable ("Devil's Bridge"), one of the oldest Romanesque bridges in France and awarded World Heritage status by UNESCO. The entrance to the "desert" is visible from the top of its parapet, almost fifty feet (15 m) above the Hérault river.

Saint-Guilhem-le-Désert owes its name to Guillaume (Guilhem in Occitan), who was count of Toulouse and duke of Aquitaine. In 804, this cousin of Charlemagne's and a redoubtable warlord decided to enter religious orders. Looking around for a remote location devoid of human presence (something called a "desert" at the time) in which to found an abbey, he alighted on the vale of the Gellone, mid-course along the Hérault, to the north of the current department of the same name. On the death of its founder in 812, the abbey adopted the name "Guilhem"; then, following his canonization in 1066, it called itself "St. Guilhem." In the Middle Ages, a piece of the True Cross, a gift from Charlemagne, attracted believers on pilgrimage to Santiago de Compostela, and the abbey became an obligatory halt. This exceptional relic was joined by others, including fragments of linen belonging to the Virgin and the remains of St. Guilhem himself. The abbey church, now the parish church, boasts the best-preserved French organ by the celebrated eighteenth-century organ-builder Jean-Pierre Cavaillé, which still accompanies Sunday service and performs in summer concerts.

*Facing page:* Ensconced in the Val de Gellone, and with the narrow lanes and flower-bedecked stone houses typical of southern France, Saint-Guilhem is recognized as one of the country's most gorgeous villages.

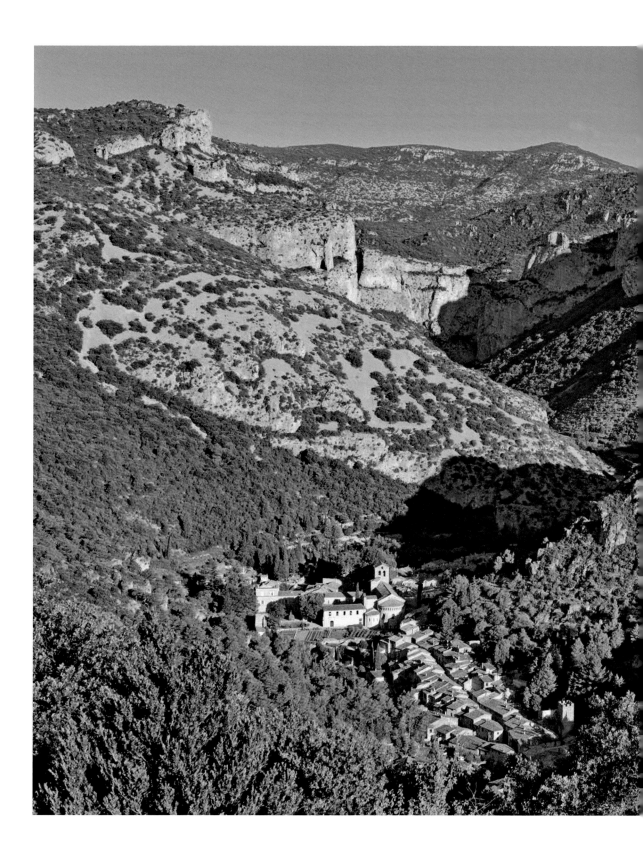

*Left*: The Val de Gellone leaves visitors awe-struck. Upstream from the village, this gully is wedged between two vertigo-inducing flanks and littered with fallen rocks.

*Above*: The abbey's organ was built in 1789 by Jean-Pierre Cavaillé, member of an important dynasty of organ-builders.

Saint-Guilhem has an air of serenity, thanks to the abbey at its center. Visitors can stroll through medieval lanes to the Place de la Liberté to enjoy the shade of a plane tree more than a hundred years old.

NICHOLAS JENNINGS, a young perfumer of English extraction, has set up a store selling organic scents in Saint-Guilhem-le-Désert. He can make up bespoke perfumes on request, using his "perfumer's organ." Working from his stone-built studio, he uses only natural products, chiefly plants from the region.

This village of 250 souls is one big happy family, whose members often meet up on the shaded square beneath an impressive plane tree more than 150 years old. With the kindness and accent typical of the Languedoc, its inhabitants are always on hand to point out to visitors one of the many undemanding walks that can be undertaken through the surrounding area. Following the stream to the corrie known as the "Bout du Monde" or to the Clamouse caverns takes scarcely more than an hour. But before you set off, they might ask you to consult the dried thistles that adorn many of the house doorways, which act as barometers. If the flower, which comes from the neighboring Larzac and is here called here the *cardabelle*, is wide open, it shouldn't rain. If it's closed, then the forecast is poor. Your guide might then urge you to visit not only the abbey museum, but also the Musée Village d'Antan: together they present a mine of information concerning the life and history of the place and its patron. Substantially damaged during the Revolution, the abbey's cloister is now in New York (the film about its journey is well worth seeing).

Foodies will doubtless enjoy the local *oreillettes*, also called *bougnettes*: succulent fritters made with dough flavored with orange flower, prepared according to a recipe passed down from generation to generation. The visitor should not leave without a quick look around the potteries, where the art of glazed ceramics has recently been revived. Saint-Jean-de-Fos, the principal center for this exquisite regional handicraft, is not far away.

*Facing page, top*: The village has grown up around the abbey. The apse of the church of Saint-Guilhem is a masterpiece of Languedoc Romanesque art.

*Right, top*: Sited in what used to be the monks' refectory, the Musée Lapidaire presents a fine collection of Romanesque and Gothic sculpture from the old abbey.

*Right, bottom*: Dried thistle, or *cardabelle*, decorates the door of many a house here. It comes from the nearby Larzac and is used as a barometer. When the thistle opens wide, as here, the forecast is good.

# VILLEFRANCHE-DE-CONFLENT

From the summit of the intact fortress, you can look down on more than ten centuries of history: Villefranche-de-Conflent's strategic position, midway between France and Spain, made it a focus of the two kingdoms' conflict for the possession of the Cerdagne (Cerdanya). Constructed out of pink marble extracted from nearby quarries, the citadel's stones bear the marks not only of the men who built it and lived here, but also those who conquered it. It is, however, "the vagrant of the Sun King" (as the Catalans called Sébastien Vauban) who left the deepest imprint.

In about 1092, the count of Cerdagne erected a fortified enclosure, creating a redoubtable stronghold between the two belligerents. Nicole, a retired history teacher, continues: "In the seventeenth century, Vauban, a military engineer of great talent in the service of Louis XIV, who had just signed the Treaty of the Pyrenees and thus gained Cerdagne, determined to reinforce this fortification through the addition of bastions. Above all, they should not be of any assistance to the Spaniards, nor give them hope that it might be retaken. The ramparts have resisted many a siege and remain unbroken. But be careful! They're a veritable maze." Vauban knew how to adapt defenses to a site's geographical position. The Fort Libéria, reached from the village by means of an underground staircase with 734 steps, forms a rough oblong. In addition, he adapted the cave of Cova Bastera on the mountainside, which dominates the town to the north. In 1669, he came to oversee the works personally. They continued throughout the eighteenth century.

*Left*: Fine ironwork on the door of the Romanesque church of Saint-Jacques.

*Facing page, top left*: The sign hanging above Marylou's bakery, which specializes in excellent *bougnettes*, or fritters flavored with orange flower.

*Facing page, top right*: The "thousand steps"— an underground passage that connects the historic center with the Fort Libéria.

*Facing page, bottom*: At the foot of the peak at Canigou, Villefranche-de-Conflent is a medieval walled town of the eleventh century, further fortified by Vauban on the orders of Louis XIV.

This medieval town, fortified by the great Vauban, is a spectacular place. Inside the fortifications, various crafts and businesses remind the visitor of its past as a trading center.

*Above and right*: The old town is still protected by its ramparts. The fortifications seen here (with the exception of the medieval towers and the walls' lower sections) are the work of Vauban; the corner bastions are characteristic of his military architecture. The space is organized around two parallel streets flanked by houses dating back to the Middle Ages, although subsequently altered at various periods.

Aside from being one of the "Most Beautiful Villages of France," this medieval settlement near Perpignan is also one of twelve locations fortified by Vauban to be recognized as UNESCO World Heritage Sites in 2008. In spite of its checkered history, this borough of 250 inhabitants, like the fort, is admirably preserved. Within its walls, the space is organized around two parallel streets: Rue Saint-Jacques to the south and Rue Saint-Jean to the north, both lined with stores and cafés (more than welcome after a stiff climb in the area). Although altered at various times, almost all the houses originally date from the Middle Ages. The twelfth-century *viguerie* (courthouse), today the town hall, occupies a corner on the church square. The church itself, dating from the foundation of Villefranche, is surmounted by a thirteenth-century belfry.

Strolling through the busy streets, the visitor risks coming across one of the famous "witches" of Conflent that the inhabitants hang at their doors to ward off evil spirits, giving them as presents to friends. With luck, you might also find Marylou's bakery, which is not to be missed. She sells succulent *bougnettes*, orange flower–scented fritters liberally sprinkled with sugar, still made by hand after an age-old recipe. "At one time, every home made them in large quantities. Some were given to neighbors, and they'd give you part of their own batch in return. This made it possible to compare each other's work and improve. There was never any meanness in these exchanges," Marylou tells us.

After one last tour around the fort and another to the caves of the Grandes Canalettes close by, you can leave Villefranche (with regret, having seen how vibrant Catalan cultural life can be) on a little yellow train, which since 1904 has connected Villefranche to the higher village of Latour-de-Carol through some breathtaking mountain scenery. Serving twenty-two stations and opening up the valley of the River Têt, the railroad is a technical marvel: its engineers designed and built no fewer than 650 structures, including 19 tunnels, over a distance of just thirty-seven miles (60 km).

This little yellow train is a great regional tourist attraction. Since 1904, it has connected Villefranche to Latour-de-Carol, passing through twenty-two stations.

# LIMOUSIN

Collonges-
la-Rouge
Turenne

BETWEEN THE AUVERGNE AND AQUITAINE, the Limousin likes to live the high life. It is a country of trees and water, a realm of anglers and canoeists, of horseriders, ramblers, and casual walkers. Its rivers are well known: the Vienne, the Creuse, the Gartempe, and the Corrèze; there is the Charente, which rises here, and the Dordogne; and also the Taurion and Vézère. There are also mountains, and the plateau of Millevaches. It is a unique place, encompassing some of the most picturesque villages in France: Collonges-la-Rouge, Curemonte, which boasts three châteaux, and Turenne in Corrèze; then you have Aubusson, renowned for its tapestries, Bourganeuf in the Creuse, and Châteauponsac in Haute-Vienne—all medieval towns where the past is etched into every stone. Granite cathedrals, and collegiate and abbey churches, such as the enormous example in Aubazine, and Bénévent-L'Abbaye, a masterpiece of Limousin Romanesque—as well as the châteaux at Turenne, Pompadour, and Rochechouart—all testify to an era when powerful local lords and the Church proclaimed their power through the construction of great monuments. The regional capital of Limoges possesses one of the most beautiful railroad stations in France, inaugurated in 1929. However, it is not to the railroad that the city and its region owe their fame, but to the porcelain produced here since the eighteenth century. The liberal economist Turgot, who at the time was *intendant* (tax collector) for the Limousin, had got wind of the discovery of kaolin at Saint-Yrieix-la-Perche and set up the Manufacture Royale de Limoges. Thus was launched a porcelain industry that soon became a leader in the art of fine tableware. Several firms continue to produce porcelain today, exporting to every continent. Yet would the Limousin really be the Limousin without the russet-colored cows that graze its meadows? This breed symbolizes both the region and its fine gastronomic tradition.

*Facing page*: A panoramic view of the Brive basin as seen from the *puy* of Yssandon, with the hills of the Périgord in the distance. The morning fog lifts to reveal an attractive, gentle landscape of meadows, moors, and coppices.

*Left*: Limousin cows, with their gorgeous fawn-colored coat, feed exclusively on grass in the open air; a sober, traditional farmhouse in the hamlet of Orlianges, in Corrèze; a rowboat waits at a river jetty.

# COLLONGES-LA-ROUGE

ome twelve miles (19 km) from Brive-la-Gaillarde, at the end of a small road bordered by horse chestnut trees, there suddenly emerges, perched on a rocky outcrop like a figurehead, a pearl of the Limousin. Surrounded by greenery and as gloriously red as the sandstone that dresses its walls, Collonges-la-Rouge stands out boldly against an azure sky. Much enamored of this architectural miracle, its five hundred residents are immensely proud to share their village with the 680,000 vacationers who visit it yearly. Turrets and watchtowers, manor houses and great mansions, pedestrian precincts and flower-bedecked lanes all speak of the small town's history and mystery. The visitor just has to look up to the pointed, slate-covered roofs to be transported to another era. Towers, pepper-pot turrets, and bartizans whisk you back to that remote time when the monks first founded a priory here, which the viscounts of Turenne took under their wing. Peasants, craftsmen, and tradesmen were soon drawn to the monastic buildings behind their fortifications. Already thriving, the community offered accommodation to pilgrims on their way to Compostela via

Rocamadour. In 1308, the borough was granted its freedom by charter of franchise and endowed with broad rights of jurisdiction. Flocks of prosecutors, lawyers, and notaries followed, who built themselves opulent homes that earned Collonges-la-Rouge the nickname "the city of twenty-five towers." The church of Saint-Pierre is equally splendid, with its gabled Romanesque bell tower, reinforced at the time of the Hundred Years War, and its entrance decorated with a tympanum in white stone, to singular effect in an otherwise crimson ensemble. It featured on a three-franc postage stamp issued in 1982.

*Top, left*: The door of the church of Saint-Pierre, surmounted by a tympanum of the twelfth century. The lower register features the eleven apostles, Judas being omitted.

*Top, right*: The top of this door knocker is in the form of a scallop shell—proof that Collonges was a stop on the way to Compostela.

*Facing page*: Collonges's dark-red houses, roofed in blue-tinged *lauzes*, back onto the thickly wooded hillside.

The Revolution was not kind to Collonges-la-Rouge, and the village would surely have fallen into disrepair without the unwavering devotion of its denizens. Conscious of its matchless beauty, in 1982 they founded the "Association of The Most Beautiful Villages of France," which is based in the Maison de la Sirène. As one enters through a Gothic doorway, the carving of a mermaid holding a comb and a mirror can be seen on the right-hand side. This sixteenth-century house once belonged to Henri de Jouvenel, Colette's second husband.

One day, more than fifteen years ago, Éric Peyronnaud moved lock, stock, and barrel to the village, and soon afterwards opened the first and only knife-making factory in the Corrèze: "A good knife, compact, solid, just like the Corrèze." After a difficult start, Éric's knives (personalized on request) became indispensable. Hillary Clinton, on a visit to the area, was presented with one of the cutler's wares, sending a thank-you letter by way of acknowledgment.

Located on the borders between the Limousin and the Périgord, Collonges-la-Rouge knows its food, and its eight restaurants make it a gastronomic paradise. Limousin lamb, duck breast, foie gras, cèpe mushroom omelet, curdled-milk tart, and chocolate and mustard cake can all be enjoyed here at their best. There are whole firms specializing in mustards: it comes in no fewer than eighteen varieties, though the most popular is the purple mustard, made using grape must. "It's really something," says Ingrid, a master mustard-producer who now incorporates the condiment in all kinds of dishes, even desserts. "It's excellent," her diners confirm, from their table on the terrace that affords a sublime view. As far as the eye can see, there's nothing but vineyards and woodland. In a shaded grove not far off is a rock with a hollow in its surface: this is meant to be the devil's seat, and legend has it that whoever dares sit on it will have their life prolonged by fifty years.

Blazingly colorful, this enchanting medieval village has a unique character.

*Pages 152–53*: Fringed by wisteria, the residence of the Ramade de la Serre dates from the sixteenth century.

*Above*: With its square tower, slender pepper-pot turret, and lych-gate, the Castel de Maussac is an early sixteenth-century manor house.

*Top*: The Halle aux Grains et aux Vins still possesses a communal oven, which is lit for the annual bread festival held on the first Sunday in August.

*Bottom, left*: An old nail-studded door awaiting restoration.

*Bottom, right*: The surrounds of the tympanum on the parish church include this carving of a bear-tamer.

# TURENNE

orn into one of its oldest families, Nicolas grew up in Turenne. Now, for the first time, he is flying over this historic village of the Corrèze in a balloon. He is struck dumb by the spectacle beneath his feet. Proudly perched on a headland that dominates the valley of the Tourmente, and protected by its feudal fortress, Turenne presents a picture of sloping slate roofs huddled around a bell tower.

For Patrick Sébastien—a native of Brive-la-Gaillarde, a neighboring town—Turenne "symbolizes all the beauty, history, and severity of the region." Now it's a tourist destination, but between the eleventh and the seventeenth centuries the village's story was somewhat unusual. Situated on an outcrop of Corrèze limestone, it owes its name to its elevated position: "Turenne" derives from the word *tonnerre*, meaning "height" in medieval Occitan. The settlement was first recorded in the ninth century, a time when the Normans would regularly make raids into France. The monks of Saint-Martial of Limoges chose Turenne— "one of the rocks best defended by nature and man"— as a good spot to keep their saints' relics out of harm's way. Turenne operated as the capital of an autonomous viscounty, whose lords raised taxes, minted currency, and convened states general. It survived as a state within the state of France until June 8, 1738, the day Charles-Godefroy de La Tour d'Auvergne, the duke of Bouillon, sold it to Louis XV to settle his gambling debts. From one day to the next, the Turennois found themselves obliged to pay royal excises, and the sovereign ordered the fortifications be dismantled. By the time of the Revolution, Turenne was no more than the seat of a royal provost.

*Above*: Proudly sited at the top of a limestone outcrop, Turenne's medieval fortress and tower look down on a verdant landscape.

*Facing page, left*: The guardroom in the ancient castle contains Louis XIII furniture and a collection of chests for storing salt.

*Facing page, right*: The tower and the gate through which people entered the village are the only surviving remnants of the medieval enclosure.

Fine, harmonious buildings,
friendly inhabitants, and excellent
regional produce together make
Turenne an ideal village.

According to local historian Jean-Pierre, the lords of neighboring lands, envious of the villagers' independence, would say that someone was "as happy as a Turennois or a Viscomtain" (both terms designated an inhabitant of Turenne). He gestures to the scenery with a sweep of his arm and invites us along for the complete tour. Climbing up to the castle along Rue Droite—the only way—he shows houses of the fifteenth century lined up as if on parade. A little farther,

the Hôtel Sclafer of the seventeenth century boasts a gallery and terraces in the Italian style. Down toward the *foirail* (marketplace) one comes across a house with a tower that belonged to the Courèze family, physicians to the *vicomtes* for generations; then Maison Crozat, apparently the viscounts' final residence; and several other, humbler abodes with stores or stone-built stalls built into the ground floor, all remarkably harmonious. The church of Notre-Dame Saint-Pantaléon, with its

octagonal bell tower, was erected during the Counter-Reformation. Henri de La Tour, lieutenant to the future Henry IV of France, had turned the viscounty into a bastion of Protestantism. When Henry IV converted to Catholicism, the rest had to follow, hence the construction of a new church. Henri de La Tour would become the "great Turenne," marshal of France and one of Louis XIV's most skillful generals. Since the original fortifications proved too small to accommodate all of the personnel required by the viscounty, hamlets (*barris*, in the local language) like the nearby Molynarie sprang up. In the cellars of the knights' houses, a few miles down the slope at the foot of the castle, tons of fossil shells have been discovered, recalling a remote period when the hill was surrounded by sea.

Yves Gary, the mayor, grew up in the hamlet of Bouzonnie. He is proud not only of his village, but also of how easygoing it is: "*Pétanque* is played seriously here. You're teased when your *boule* misses the target. That's part of the game. And being trustful doesn't mean that you don't check," he notes, before speaking about the truffle, another pretext for sharing pleasure with his friends. Patrick Sébastien likes to eat his in an omelet at the château of Coutinard. "I've often found myself here, sitting at a table; above and beyond the delicious meal, there are the people, friendly and very down-to-earth." You can almost hear the burghers of Turenne burst into applause.

*Facing page, top:* At the beginning of the Rue de l'Église, the Maison des Chanoines—an elegant sixteenth-century residence with a splendid Gothic doorway—has been converted into a boutique hotel and restaurant.

*Facing page, bottom:* A sloping street in Turenne, bordered by closely packed houses.

*Left, top:* Along the narrow Rue Droite, these houses, enlarged in the seventeenth century, have thick walls of honey-colored stone. Leading from the market on the Place de la Halle, it is the only way to access the fortress.

*Left, bottom:* The octagonal bell tower of the collegiate church of Notre-Dame Saint-Pantaléon, built in a sober Romanesque style, emerges above the village rooftops.

# LORRAINE

ONE HOUR AND THIRTY MINUTES from Paris by high-speed train, Lorraine, industrial to the north, but agrarian and rural to the south, shares a border with Belgium, Luxembourg, and Germany. Approximately sixty miles (100 km) across, the territory lies between the forests of the Argonne and the massif of the Vosges. Rich in lakes, including the Lac de Gérardmer, and in thermal spas such as those at Contrexéville, Plombières, and Vittel, it is also the most wooded region in all France. A hilly country, it is a center for many different sports and leisure activities: alpine and cross-country skiing, ski-touring in the Bresse (the largest skiable area in the Vosges), rambling, mountain-biking, and horseriding along nearly 10,000 miles (16,000 km) of signposted paths, including the Transvosgienne. Owing to its position at the crux of many conflicts between European states, Lorraine has a checkered history somewhat different from that of the rest of France, and its built heritage has been shaped by cultural and economic interactions. Wars left deep marks, in the form of the Maginot Line's forts and the American cemetery at Saint-Avold, but also châteaux, such as those at Malbrouck and Lunéville. Forged by such ordeals, its cities have acquired a strong personality: Nancy, with its famous Place Stanislas, is a heartland of Art Nouveau; Metz, adorned in a symphony of yellow, ocher, and bronze, benefits from a pedestrianized center encompassing its marvelous cathedral and the Pompidou-Metz art center; Bar-le-Duc, proud of its position at the beginning of the Sacred Way that leads to Verdun, with its painful memories of wholesale slaughter; and Épinal, as traditional as the popular colored prints that bore its name in the nineteenth century. It is also a place where the beautiful and the useful go hand in hand: there is a celebrated school of arts and crafts in Nancy, enamel and earthenware are worked at Sarreguemines and Lunéville, and the crystal glass of Baccarat is world famous.

*Facing page*: The Vosges mountains—which in wintertime are usually draped in snow—are a paradise for hikers and nature lovers in any season.

*Left*: The mirabelle, the golden plum of the Lorraine, is a highlight of many festivals; unsophisticated but colorful, the prints known as *images d'Épinal* were highly popular in the nineteenth century; these lead soldiers bring to mind the 1916 Battle of Verdun, one of the most murderous of World War I.

# RODEMACK

In this land of three borders, Rodemack perches on a green hill twelve miles (20 km) from Germany and three-and-a-half miles (6 km) from Luxembourg. Known as the "little Carcassonne" of Lorraine and a listed historic monument, the village is still encircled by 2,300 feet (700 m) of ramparts dating from the fifteenth century. You enter through the reinforced Porte de Sierck, built in the sixteenth century to ward off attack. This medieval village is like a time capsule: there are only four stores. You don't come here to go shopping, but to admire the exceptional built heritage.

Like any local worth her salt, Geneviève de Fontenay says she is "mad about Rodemack." And she's not alone.

Philippe Lelong, a teacher, moved here ten years ago, falling in love with both the village and a girl from the village. Thirty years ago, neglected and abandoned, this "little Carcassonne" was a sorry sight. As Jean-Marie Pelt, a founder member of the European Institute of Ecology and a local, wrote: "For centuries Rodemack's ramparts and fortresses had been used as a quarry from which building stone was taken in liberal quantities. One day, Rodemack rubbed its eyes and woke up. Suddenly people thought about this medieval fortress, standing solidly there on the Hettangian faultline, with its vaulted cellars, its covered ways, its oubliettes.... People harked back to a time when the enclosing wall had been almost intact.... This became the focus of a

*Facing page*: Nicknamed the "little Carcassonne of the Lorraine," the village of Rodemack is still protected behind fifteenth-century walls. It is entered via a fortified gateway, the Porte de Sierck, built by the inhabitants themselves.

*Above, left*: Restored under the aegis of a local association, the Amis des Vieilles Pierres ("Friends of the Old Stones"), the old washhouse has had its roof replaced and is now decorated with flowers.

*Above, right*: Like all the footpaths skirting the ramparts, the Ruelle de la Grimpette has kept all its period charm and makes for an enchanting walk.

new life for the village. . . . Festivals and traditions were reborn, filling the streets with life and color. Worksites sprang up. Then came the crowning glory: the village was accepted into the exclusive club of the 'Most Beautiful Villages of France.'"

That's pretty much the situation today. Everyone puts his shoulder to the wheel. One weekend a month, all the Rodemackois can be found shoring up or restoring the ramparts in programs organized by the "Friends of the Old Stones." Fabien Marien never misses a weekend. He and his wife (a local) bought a house in the village they are now renovating. Franck Morisseau, who has been dealing with the association's restoration sites since 2006, tells a similar story. Locals are especially attached to the church of Saint-Nicolas, the Maison des Baillis, constructed in 1560, the old post office, the washhouse, and the presbytery built in 1736 (a date inscribed on the key). The majestic Porte de Sierck, the very symbol of Rodemack, was destroyed during World War II, but the inhabitants themselves rebuilt it according to a drawing by Victor Hugo. The village's narrow streets—including the oldest of them all, the Ruelle de la Forge—are full of life. About four hundred lucky souls live within the village walls, and all feel at home.

Like Philippe, the teacher who often brings his pupils here, visitors like to venture into the bowels of the fortress and climb to the top of the ramparts. The Terrasse des Officiers provides the best view. From up there, the eye can see for miles—a useful vantage point for Philippe's history class to learn about geography and medieval strategy. To round off the visit, you should not miss the medieval garden, planted in 1990 on a narrow plot of land between the ramparts and the Ruisseau des Oiseaux. An ongoing project, it resembles the *hortus conclusus* (enclosed garden) frequently found in medieval forts. The planted areas are arranged geometrically, the beds, which are higher than the walkways connecting them, being separated off by low

I am 'godfather' to the town of Rodemack, and that's why I am totally committed to supporting the local volunteers who work tirelessly to restore the heritage of this fortified commune.

walls. The garden is shared equally between medicinal plants, condiments, herbs and spices, flowers, vegetables, and food and other utility crops. The whole garden is organized and maintained by an education project in partnership with the vocational college of La Briquerie, and won a national prize from the Ford Foundation.

Every summer, Rodemack organizes a medieval fete, complete with shows and a procession of knights. It is then that the village returns entirely to the feudal age.

*Facing page, top*: The chapel of Notre-Dame was erected in 1658 by the population of Rodemack to thank the Virgin for her intercession during plague epidemics and for the return of peace.

*Facing page, bottom*: The attractive yellow façade and blue shutters of the old post office, covered in geraniums.

*Above, top*: The sign hanging over the Maison des Baillis, built in 1560 to house the bailiff who wielded authority over the village in the name of the local ruler.

*Above, bottom*: A view of the citadel, its ramparts, and the park planted in the nineteenth century.

# SAINT-QUIRIN

On the first spurs of the Vosges, Saint-Quirin in the Moselle, classified as one of the "Most Beautiful Villages of France," nestles in a verdant bower. Located fifty miles (80 km) from Nancy, it is a small town of eight hundred inhabitants that owes its name to a Roman tribune, Quirinus, who was martyred in the second century CE. Traces of the Roman settlement have been unearthed at the archeological site of Croix-Guillaume, just outside the village.

Huddled around a priory owned by the abbey at Marmoutier, for a long time Saint-Quirin was an important center of pilgrimage. According to legend, the relics of St. Quirinus, tortured in 132 in Rome under the reign of Emperor Hadrian, were brought here in 1049 by Geppa, the abbess of Neuss and a sister of Pope Leo IX. The mule carrying them halted on the slope above the village, at the site of the current Chapelle Haute. The precious relics were stored there for a time before being deposited in the priory church. Regularly and radically altered, today the chapel has been reduced to a patchwork—except for the chancel and the bell tower, which preserve a measure of homogeneity. Built in the pinkish sandstone of the Vosges, it takes the form of a rectangle fifty feet (15 m) long and eighteen feet (5.6 m) wide with an aisleless nave.

*Facing page*: The priory church of Saint-Quirin, with its three onion-domed towers. In the background is the Chapelle Haute, the second most important religious building in the village.

*Above, left*: The statue of St. Quirinus, patron saint of the village, looks over a miraculous spring whose water is said to cure skin diseases.

*Above, right*: A view from one of the many footpaths in the area.

The priory church (now the parish church) was dedicated in 1123 and destroyed during the Thirty Years War. Rebuilt in 1722 in a typical baroque style, it is surmounted by three onion-domed towers—two with a triple "onion." Its many treasures include the only surviving organ in Lorraine (installed in 1746 and restored in 1969) by the great maker Jean-André Silbermann. "For me, it is an enormous privilege to be able to play such an instrument, a listed historic monument. I was just eighteen the first time I placed my hands on its keyboards. I felt very humble and very small. It is this instrument that gives the tempo to each service. It belongs to the history of the people here, to their DNA," enthuses Christophe, the organist who has accompanied every religious festival here since he was a young

man. Each year, the relics of St. Quirinus are borne in a great procession from the church to the chapel. "We follow in the footsteps of all those who, for centuries, have gathered there and gazed down on their valley. The soul of the village is up there, a place where human and natural heritage blend in such harmony," Pierre, the manager of the Sainte-Croix safari park and a resident of Saint-Quirin for fifteen years, remarks. Along with five other religious buildings of great beauty scattered about the neighboring communes, these two monuments form an ensemble known as the "seven roses." Skirting around the vicarage next to the church, the visitor comes across the "miraculous fountain," whose water is (apparently) a panacea for skin diseases.

In the hamlet of Lettenbach, a little off the beaten track, a glassmaking factory founded in the fifteenth century was active for four centuries. Storehouses, workmen's cottages, underground galleries, the furnace, and a chapel—erected for the employees' use in 1756, using stained glass made on site—testify to the business's importance. The furnace was responsible for the mirrors that adorn the palace of the dukes of Lorraine in Nancy, and it was accorded a patent as a royal manufactory by Louis XV.

Many marked paths leave from the village—a center for outdoor recreation—through the area's extensive forests. On foot, mountain bike, or horseback, they offer a great opportunity to observe animals, plants, and even large game that the butcher of Saint-Quirin turns into succulent specialties. At the Hostellerie du Prieuré, Didier and Valérie Soulier will treat lovers of traditional cuisine to *truite meunière* cooked with almonds or in Riesling, fresh fish from the ponds, and mirabelle plums, known as the "queen of the Moselle."

Saint-Quirin will appeal to those
interested in ecclesiastical history.
Nature lovers, too, will enjoy the many
hiking trails that lead off into the Vosges.

*Facing page*: The only surviving
organ in the Lorraine by the great
organ-builder Jean-André
Silbermann. It was first installed
in the priory church in 1746.

*Above*: The glassmaking factory
in the hamlet of Lettenbach,
founded in the fifteenth century.
Louis XV accorded it the status of
royal manufactory. The smaller
building facing the green is the
glassmakers' chapel.

*Right*: The doorway to the priory,
surmounted by an elaborate
baroque pediment.

# MIDI-PYRÉNÉES

THE MIDI-PYRÉNÉES REGION coincides with Occitania—the Pays d'Oc, a land forced to be part of France against its will. Here there were two sister languages, Gascon and Languedocian, which fused into one: the language of the troubadours. It's a land of sunshine, skittish and voluble, as firmly attached to its age-old ways of life as to its accent. It arose from the clash between a venerable mountain range to the north, and a young upstart in the south. As the Pyrenees heaved, the Massif Central rose and split into plateaus, between which run the great rivers of the Lot, the Aveyron, and the Tarn. Often deep-sided, their valleys separate or link plains and hills, each with its own, very different scenery and produce. The smallest hill bears a brick-built town, whose origins often date back to medieval times, complete with checkerboard thirteenth-century *bastides* around a central square, in accordance with the usual urban plan of the period. It is at the intersection of eight departments—on the plain of Toulouse irrigated by the Garonne and extending southeast along the slopes of the Lauragais, and westward into the hills of the Gers—that the vines that make Armagnac are grown. The whole region is a successful blend of two opposing temperaments: the inhabitants keep to themselves in the Massif Central, while toward the Pyrenees they are prouder. "Toulouse the Pink" is a synthesis: a university metropolis, cosmopolitan and dynamic, and a regional capital boasting a wealth of enterprise and advanced technology. The enduring dream of the Midi-Pyrénées has always been to link the Mediterranean to the Atlantic, however. Pierre-Paul Riquet almost made it a reality in the seventeenth century, when he connected Sète with Toulouse via the Canal du Midi, which now extends toward Bordeaux as a side channel of the Garonne. The Bordeaux country bequeathed rugby to the region, which here is both a sport and a way of life: victories are celebrated with foie gras, and defeats commiserated at legendary get-togethers.

*Facing page*: Erected in the nineteenth century, the circular cairns up on the Pailhères pass have been recently restored.

*Left*: Rocamadour, in the Haut-Quercy, is a medieval walled town firmly attached to the cliffside; a colorful façade in Montauban; the Place du Capitole in Toulouse has two nameplates, one in French and one in Occitan.

# CONQUES

onques is a tiny village—but what a site! To the north of Rodez, nestling at the bottom of a wooded cirque, it lies at the confluence of the Dourdou and the Ouche. Its surroundings form a kind of shell—in Latin *concha*—hence the name. The medieval village appears at a bend in a minor road, halfway up a sun-kissed slope and coiled around its abbey of Sainte-Foy. Here, schist is king. It provides not only building stone, but also paving for the streets, and *lauze* tiles for the roofs. For windows and doorframes, however, masons tended to prefer a pinkish or gray sandstone. The resulting ocher hue of the village, with its iridescent, rosy highlights, is in perfect keeping with the natural environment. This pocket paradise numbers about 282 inhabitants, but 600,000 visitors walk through it every year. The popularity of Conques comes as no surprise:

the Midi-Pyrénées has classified it as one the region's most important sites; UNESCO has placed the abbey—a jewel of Romanesque art—on its World Heritage list; and the village is recognized as a major stopover on the pilgrims' route to Compostela.

The abbey church of Sainte-Foy (St. Faith) is the most obvious attraction. Every day Brother Jean-Daniel, a member of the community and often to be found seated at the organ, tells the story of the foundation: descending from Puy-en-Velay, pilgrims entered the wild country of the Aubrac toward the valley of the Lot. Halting at Conques, they found the relics of St. Faith, transported there from Agen in 866, in the church. Many walkers still take this historic route, using the village as a staging point and sometimes choosing to take lodgings in the monastery's guest quarters. Damaged during the Wars of Religion, abandoned at the Revolution, and

*Facing page, left*: Brother Jean-Daniel playing the organ in the abbey of Sainte-Foy, a masterpiece of Romanesque art built between the eleventh and twelfth centuries.

*Facing page, right*: A reliquary statue of St. Foy (St. Faith) dating to the ninth century—the centerpiece of the abbey's treasury, housed in the abbey's cloister.

*Above*: The peerless abbey church of Sainte-Foy in Conques receives some 600,000 visitors a year.

*Top*: The old fountain at the center of the abbey's cloister, carved out of serpentine.

*Bottom, left*: One of the windows designed by Pierre Soulages. Made from translucent, colorless glass, they both preserve and modulate natural light entering the abbey.

*Bottom, right*: An inquisitive face peers out from the twelfth-century tympanum of the Last Judgment on the west door.

*Facing page*: Halfway up the hillside facing the sun, the village is ablaze with hues of pink and ocher, in perfect harmony with its surroundings.

There's so much to admire and
enjoy here. Nothing disturbs
the village's majesty or serenity.

earmarked for destruction, the abbey—and its splendid tympanum of the Last Judgment, complete with 124 intact figures over nine centuries old—was rediscovered in 1837. Its was spotted by the author of *Carmen*, Prosper Mérimée, at that time the general inspector of historic buildings, who secured the necessary funds for its restoration. The works continued for more than a century and were completed in 1994 with the installation of new stained-glass windows, designed, executed, and put in place by a great painter from the Aveyron, Pierre Soulages.

The abbey's treasury, which is open to the public, displays the reliquary statue of St. Foy—made of gold and studded with precious stones donated by pilgrims—alongside other masterpieces of medieval goldwork. One passing pilgrim, Pascal, who claims to be averaging about twenty-two miles (35 km) a day, halts at the entrance to the village, on the bridge over the Dourdou (known as the "Roman" bridge), before climbing toward the chapel of Sainte-Foy and its miraculous spring. "Apparently it gives the blind their sight back. For me, I'm just hoping it will make the world look more beautiful," he says with a laugh, rubbing his eyes. The village also harbors more material treasures,

as well as excellent sustenance for the flesh. Opposite the pilgrims' fountain, the Musée Joseph Fau displays a sumptuous collection of tapestries and furniture. Painters, an antiques dealer, an engraver, a soapmaker, a woodcarver, a stonemason, and a tapestry-weaver have all opened up shop here.

Prince Charles once visited and erected his easel, but it is not known whether he tackled the panorama from Bancarel, whence the view over Conques is unique; nor whether he snatched a little something at the restaurant in the Moulin de Cambelong, where they once extracted oil from sweet chestnuts. Michelin-starred chef Hervé Busset concocts regional specialties in the hotel's restaurant—including a giant doughnut, the *fouace*—and recommends local wines produced by Patrick Rols, a distant heir to the winemaking monks.

# SAINT-CIRQ-LAPOPIE

Saint-Cirq-Lapopie has been contemplating the valley of the Lot from the top of its cliff for centuries. The Gallo-Romans, and perhaps even prehistoric people before them, are known to have been attracted to this rocky headland between earth and sky. Anyone and everyone who stops at this place, seventeen miles (30 km) from Cahors, in the center of the regional nature reserve of the Causses de Quercy, is struck by its beauty. The founder of Surrealism, André Breton, never really recovered from the impression he received one evening in June 1950. "Ablaze with Bengal fires, Saint-Cirq appeared to me as an impossible rose in the nighttime. Next morning I returned, tempted to settle in the heart of this flower.... I stopped wanting to be elsewhere," he wrote, and went on to acquire the old Auberge des Mariniers. Until the nineteenth century, the area was mainly supplied by river traffic, a once vanished means of transport that has now reappeared in the form of pleasure craft. A walk down the towpath, with its wonderfully picturesque backdrop, gives one a good idea of the trade that must once have flourished on the river.

Up steep lanes lined with houses dating from the Middle Ages, whose charm is enhanced by their perfectly maintained corbels and steep-pitched roofs, the visitor reaches a plateau crowned by three ruined castles and a church fortified by a square bell tower and a turret with a staircase—illustrious evidence of a chivalric period and the reach of royal politics. In 1471, Louis XI ordered the demolition of the castle of Raymond de Cardaillac, the local lord; under Charles VIII, Raymond had it rebuilt with the compensation he received for the damage inflicted during the preceding reign. The whole ensemble is dominated by the impressive

*Above*: The plateau above Saint-Cirq is reached via steep lanes lined with tile-roofed medieval houses.

*Facing page, bottom*: A bas-relief by sculptor Daniel Monnier on the banks of the River Lot, where the *gabarres* are moored.

*Left*: A softly lit restaurant terrace on a mild summer's evening.

Saint-Cirq-Lapopie was the first to be voted 'France's Favorite Village,' in 2012. What an amazing party we had that evening!

fortified Gothic church, which overlooks the village's picturesque arcades, brown-tiled houses, workshops with wooden frontages, intriguing doorways, and steep side streets. Now a frequent stopover on the pilgrim route to Compostela and one of the most visited locations in the Midi-Pyrénées, Saint-Cirq-Lapopie used to boast a powerful guild of woodturners, whose skill is perpetuated by two working craftsmen. As well as the turners, the village's wealth came from its leather-workers and ironmongers; today these activities are being revived in active workshops and by means of a museum. Artists' residencies and exhibitions are arranged by the Maisons Daura, dwellings once occupied by the painter Pierre Daura—an endeavor in which the village's residents engage enthusiastically.

*Pages 178–79*: From the top of a cliff, Saint-Cirq-Lapopie and its fortified church have surveyed the River Lot since time immemorial.

*Above, left*: A portrait of André Breton, the founder of Surrealism, carved by Pierre Daura on the writer's house.

*Above, right*: Traditional handicrafts are still produced by potters, woodturners, ironmongers, and other local craftsmen.

The Château de la Gardette, once a
bastion occupied by the advanced
guard, now houses the Musée
Rignault and its many works of art.

PATRICK VINEL, a woodturner
in Saint-Cirq-Lapopie, is
the last in a dynasty of five
generations of tappers and
woodturners, and the only
person in the village to practice
this traditional craft. He has a
workshop on the main street,
which, come high season, is
always full of tourists eager
to discover this local skill.

# NORD-
# PAS-DE-CALAIS

Wissant
Maroilles

THE NORD-PAS-DE-CALAIS is a land of vast skies, long beaches, soft light, and endless plains. Facing the nearby English coast and close to Belgium, its great spaces open onto the North Sea, which has been gnawing away at them since time began. The plains in which the Scarpe, the Lys, and the Aa have dug out their clayey beds, dotted about with hills, can be read like a history book. In 1803, from the top of Mont Cassel, which looks down on Flanders, Napoleon took time from a busy campaign to exclaim: "This is a view of the most splendid picture nature ever drew in a lowland country." It is a mosaic of treeless or wooded territories, in which every accident of the terrain leaps out, adding to its charm. It is crisscrossed by a dense network of canals—those of Calais, the Scheldt, and the Sambre à l'Oise, plus the Canal du Nord—that connect its cities to those of Belgium and the Netherlands. The region was strategically important for Charles V and Louis XIV, and in the nineteenth century was also a significant economic hub—a role supplemented more recently by the development of tourism along the waterways. The architecture is fashioned essentially from cob, brick, timber, sandstone, the "blue stone" of the Avesnois, white stone from the Artois, tile, and, especially, slate. The mining cottages and workers' houses immortalized by Zola in *Germinal* testify to a long industrial past centered around collieries and textile factories. Not many cities marry past, present, and future as completely as the regional capital, Lille, whose metropolitan area contains a population of more than one million. The varied façades on the Grand-Place are the result of Flemish, Burgundian, and Spanish influences. The city has recently gained in prominence as a stop on the high-speed train link between London, Paris, and Brussels.

*Facing page*: The world kite-flying festival at Berck-sur-Mer—a colorful aerial ballet held in a festive atmosphere.

*Left*: The Dunkirk carnival attracts an immense, colorful crowd in fancy dress; the decorative baroque gables on the Place d'Arras betray a Flemish influence; the unmissable *estaminet*—a traditional watering hole in which villagers like to meet up and relax.

# MAROILLES

Mention the word "Maroilles," and most French people think you're talking about a square cow's-milk cheese with an orange crust, a creamy texture, and a somewhat persistent aroma. In this case, however, we are concerned with Maroilles-en-Thiérache, the village that gave the cheese its name, thus bringing it worldwide fame. People come here from far and wide, for the cheese, of course, but also because it's such a beautiful place. Located in the nature reserve of the Avesnois, twenty-three miles (37 km) from Valenciennes and ensconced in meadows crossed by rivers, it is a typical town of the Nord, with its red-brick houses, a baroque church, and an (occasionally) cloudless sky. It preserves the remains of a substantial abbey, founded in 652 by St. Humbert, which enjoyed a succession of sixty-eight abbots and held sway over the Hainaut for a millennium. To build the abbey, they took stone from a large clearing called, in the dialect of the time, a *maroialo*, hence the village's current name.

The abbey did not survive the Revolution, but the parish church has inherited its organ, ordered from the Lille organ-builder Antoine Gaubert in 1725. The instrument, which is equipped with four manuals and thirty-nine stops, has an exceptional sound, and regularly features in concerts and recordings of baroque music, especially pieces by Couperin. Opposite the town hall, which long ago put up the *bailli*, who represented seignorial authority, is the former dwelling of the extern brother, now converted into the tourist office. The village's narrow streets lead to the tithe barn where the peasants would deposit the taxes they owed to the monks. Today, exhibitions are regularly organized here. A brick-and-stone staircase leads to the mill, which since the seventeenth century has jauntily straddled the Helpe Mineure, a river teeming with fish. The lintel over the doorway still bears the motto of Frédéric d'Yves: *Adherere Deo bonum est*, or in other words, "It is good to be close to God."

*Facing page*: In 1995, the abbey's seventeenth-century watermill on the banks of the Helpe Mineure was fitted with a new waterwheel, similar to the one that must have turned when France was still a monarchy.

*Left*: Often served at bars accompanied by a glass of beer, *flamiche* with Maroilles cheese is an authentic *Ch'ti* (or "Northern") recipe.

Pastoral, bucolic, festive, delectable:
just some of the adjectives used
to describe this friendly little town.

Daniel Druesnes, known as Dany de Maroilles, the only cheese producer in the village, delivers to the local stores and restaurants every day. As Hervé—the local historian who, like the 1,500 other Maroillais, adores his village—explains: "Our famous cheese is supposed to have been invented in the abbey in the tenth century.... It's no spring chicken, the Maroilles! The time it needs to ripen in a damp cellar is laid down in an ordinance of 1174. It is said that it delighted royal taste buds, from Charles V to Francis I." Dany is also a fan, and can't see why, in future tastings, celebrities shouldn't replace kings as famous patrons. In 2001, he took over the farm at Cerfmont together with his wife.

While his son tends the animals and his daughter-in-law churns the cheese, he and his wife sell at market and to regional hotels. There's also passing trade from visitors who are delighted to take home a cheese that has been matured on the farm for at least three weeks (and often much longer). Maroilles is an AOC (origin-controlled) product—the only one in a region that boasts some thirty varieties. Dany and Hervé agree that you just cannot visit their beautiful village without trying *flamiche* made with Maroilles cheese: a sort of oven-baked tart laced with fresh cream and covered in chunky slices of Maroilles. The odor it gives off during baking might be powerful, but the taste is not so strong: "just right," as the cognoscenti put it. Back in the village, the sound of the bell tower chiming the tune of "Le P'tit Quinquin" (the anthem of the *Ch'tis*, or "Northerners") is the call to lunch, and no meal worthy of the name can be served without the local cheese and an apple from the Avesnois. On Sundays, a tot of *genièvre* (jenever) is welcome, as it is on occasions such as the flea market, which is held on the third Sunday in June and stretches for more than three and a half miles (6 km) in total.

To burn off the calories, the men of the village go off to tickle pike from the banks of the river. After that, it's better not to disturb the *p'tits gars*, except if you want to admire their catch. "That's how the *Ch'tis* are. Stand-offish at the outset, but with hearts of gold." It is not for nothing that the sociability and friendliness of the Nord has become proverbial.

*Top*: Delicious Maroilles cheese, a local specialty.

*Left*: The parish church of Saint-Humbert was built in brick and blue stone between 1729 and 1738. The porch is decorated with fine scrollwork.

Top: The bandstand on the village green. This open space was drained, leveled, and planted with a hundred lime trees in 1808.

Bottom, left: Inside the church of Saint-Humbert. The oak paneling in the choir is the work of the Troyaux brothers, local carpenters who were active in the eighteenth century.

Bottom, right: A painting representing St. Humbert, who founded the abbey and the village in 680. His relics are kept in a copper-gilt reliquary in the church.

*Above*: The Côte d'Opale owes its
name to the milk-white stone
from which fishermen's cottages
such as this were built.

*Facing page*: Favorable winds
make the beach at Wissant
one of the best spots in Europe
for kite- and windsurfing.
The Cap Blanc-Nez rises
in the background.

# WISSANT

Wissant has become a favorite spot with windsurfers. Usually favorable winds, and the nearby Calais-Fréthun high-speed station, have encouraged sailboarders and kite-surfers to flock here from all over the world. Looking along miles of fine, sandy beach, anyone can spot a sail—or, more often, several—careering through the skies. Wissant is the ideal place to learn any board-sport. "The bay is magnificent. It's one of the best spots in Europe to train in kiteboard and windsurf. It's really an exceptional place," says Jules Denel, an adventurer from Lille with ocean-blue eyes and long, fair hair. Aged only twenty-two, he is already twice junior world champion and twice national champion in windsurfing.

This ancient little town on the shores of the Côte d'Opale occupies a bay between two cliffs, protected to the south by the Cap Gris-Nez—the stretch of

French coastline nearest to England—and to the north by the Cap Blanc-Nez, the northernmost in all France. General de Gaulle liked to spend his vacations at this small seaside resort and would often go for walks here. Some old-timers still remember seeing him inhaling the iodine-rich sea air. "Everything is beautiful in Wissant, and the people are as nice as they could possibly be. They are the soul of the village," say a few locals seated at a table in Le Charlemagne, the village bar. It's midday. Time for a snifter. Selling the fish from the morning's catch is over for the day, and Myriam is packing away her stall.

The *flobart*, the traditional craft on the Côte d'Opale, measures between thirteen and sixteen-and-a-half feet (4 and 5 m) long. Flat-bottomed and lacking a keel, it is easy to beach. Designed to be launched directly from the strand, the broad, easily maneuverable *flobarts* have fished these coastal waters since the seventeenth century, and can bring in catches of up to two

A highly attractive seaside village that has managed to preserve
its original character and environment. The fishermen
still celebrate a yearly festival of the *flobart*: a traditional,
flat-bottomed boat that used to be hauled ashore by horse.

YVES MALFOY, the grandson of a fisherman, comes from true Wissantais stock. A great promoter of his village, he has worked for the local authority for thirty-three years and manages Wissant's municipal campsite.

tons. Nowadays they are pulled onto the sand by tractor, though formerly it was men or draft horses from the Boulonnais, with their characteristic white coats and sturdy chests, that did the hauling. Wissant pays due homage to these animals every year in the last weekend in August, with a procession, music, and sea shanties.

Backing onto marshland protected behind a slender band of dunes, this village of a thousand inhabitants is centered around a church that shelters a statue of St. Wilgeforte, a bearded female martyr of the eleventh century. To prevent her father marrying her against her will and to give her suitors second thoughts, heaven furnished her face with a goodly set of whiskers. Enraged, her father promptly had her crucified. Capped with red roofs and built in the milk-white stone that gave the "Opal Coast" its name, fishermen's cottages stand in terraces. For centuries, Wissant lived for the most part from the bounty of the sea. Several archeological digs along the coast have revealed the signs of ancient occupation but have not yet unearthed the famous Portus Itius, mentioned by Julius Caesar in Book VII of his *Gallic Wars*, that many believe stood here. No matter: along the road to Calais, an old medieval earthen fortress with two enclosures is still called "Caesar's Camp" to this day. Until the sixteenth century it served as the principal port for ships sailing to England, but it increasingly became silted up and ceded this role to Calais.

Between beach and woodland, in the heart of a natural park of capes and marshes, Wissant was a magnet to director Claude Lelouch, who shot several scenes of his road movie *In the Affirmative* here. Before him, many painters had fallen for the gentle light of this "wild pearl." In the second half of the nineteenth century, the artist Adrien Demont and his partner, Virginie Demont-Breton, settled and entertained their friends here. In 1891, they built a villa, called Le Typhonium, in a neo-Egyptian style, despite never having been to Egypt. Now a listed historic building, it was instrumental in gaining the bay its official status as a site of national importance. Until the 1930s, the couple and twenty-five of their artist friends formed the "School of Wissant": realist painters who immortalized the village's fishermen, moors, and beachfront in their works.

*Facing page, top*: Situated between two cliffs on the part of the French coast closest to England, the Bay of Wissant boasts over seven miles (12 km) of fine, sandy beach.

*Facing page, bottom*: A *flobart*—a traditional fishing boat that can be hauled onto the beach—returns to port with its catch.

*Top, left*: The River Herlen winds through the village before emptying into the sea.

*Top, right*: A veritable institution in Wissant, the Hôtel de la Plage has belonged to the same family for generations. It is one of the oldest hotels on the Côte d'Opale.

# PAYS-DE-LA-LOIRE

Sainte-Suzanne
Montsoreau

THE PERCHE, MAINE, ANJOU, THE VENDÉE, the area around Nantes—the River Loire brings them all together, serving as their backbone and opening them up to the ocean. Nantes, Angers, Saumur, Baugé, Brissac, and Fontevraud are all places that have played a significant role in the histories of France and England, during the period when both were under the sway of the Plantagenets. The aristocracy commissioned fortified castles or elegant châteaux; the Church constructed its powerful abbeys; rich bourgeois built desirable residences for their families; and smallholders gave their houses sober but often elegant façades. Ample building material could be had on the spot: granite, schist, limestone, slate. In Anjou and in the valley of the Loir, men even dug rows of dwellings out of the tuffeau slopes. On the Atlantic coast, around Saint-Nazaire and Pornic, and along coastal rivers, oyster farmers and fishermen built their huts on piles, creating fisheries that are now a favorite with tourists. Agriculture and stockbreeding are of the highest quality here, and have spawned a refined gastronomy: *mâche* salad leaves from Nantes, the rosé wines of Anjou, Guérande rock salt, mushrooms from Saumur, "Petit LU" biscuits, duck from Challans, the juicy *doyenne du comice* pear, and the *rouge des prés* (a breed of cattle with a reddish pied coat). Here, a time-honored *savoir faire* informs a traditional cuisine in keeping with the environment, respectful of the ingredients' flavor, and availing itself of "boat-fresh" produce from the sea. Every worthwhile meal is washed down—moderately needless to say—with wines from Anjou, the Saumur area, or the Coteaux du Loir.

*Facing page*: The castle of La Bretesche, in Missillac in the Loire-Atlantique, was built in the purest Gothic style in the fourteenth and fifteenth centuries, and was restored in the nineteenth.

*Left*: Trawler nets drying in the port of La Turballe; a typical thatched-roof house in the heart of the Brière nature reserve; saltpans on the Île d'Olonne.

# MONTSOREAU

"You can succumb to the charm of Montsoreau at any time," declares Laurence Laboutière, who has lived happily in this village in the Maine-et-Loire, between Chinon and Saumur, for about fifteen years. "I wouldn't leave it for anything. At seven o'clock in the morning, the sunrise over the Loire takes the breath away. Here, I feel at one with nature. Every day, every morning, every evening, I am delighted to rediscover this piece of tuffeau that enhances the colors of every flower," she enthuses, her gaze lost over the majestic river that bestows such irresistible charm and softness on this little town.

Montsoreau owes much to the Loire running at its feet, which as early as the Middle Ages was already contributing to its development. A bustling port, it was the site of large markets where wheat from the area around Loudun, and wines from the Chinon region and Poitou, were bought and sold, and then ferried by inland waterway to Nantes. By the fifteenth century, its lord had become sufficiently wealthy—partly thanks to a toll imposed on the river traffic—to build himself one of the first pleasure palaces in the whole region. Conserving its fortified aspect to the north, to the south this impressive château displays an elegant façade of Italian Renaissance inspiration. It opened to the public at the beginning of the twentieth century, and since 2001 had also presented a history-themed son et lumière. It should come as no surprise that the village and its château—perhaps at its most moving and romantic enveloped in morning mist rising from the Loire—inspired a novel by Alexandre Dumas: *La Dame de Monsoreau* (the "t" was deliberately omitted),

*Above:* The village of Montsoreau and its elegant château at the confluence of the Vienne and the Loire.

*Facing page, left:* The château frequently stages son-et-lumière shows that tell the true story of *La Dame de Monsoreau.*

*Facing page, right:* At Le Saut-aux-Loups, a group of troglodyte dwellings dating to the fifteenth century is well worth a visit.

66 Montsoreau has many highlights: a château straight out of a fairy tale, flowery lanes, troglodyte caves, mushroom beds, watermills, and, for those so inclined, the wines of the Loire. 99

*Right, top*: Hollyhocks growing in front of a traditional tuffeau-stone house with blue shutters.

*Right, bottom*: The south front of the château, inspired by the Italian Renaissance, with an elegant tower housing its main staircase.

village houses are constructed is a "miracle stone," a dream to work with, and was extracted in the nineteenth century on a large scale from quarries on the local hillsides. Montsoreau experienced a rise in population, from 600 to more than 1,000, before the stone began to run out and the number of inhabitants fell back to around 480, where it stands today. The galleries dug out at Le Saut-aux-Loups (the "Wolf Leap"), reached along a knot of pathways, have been cleverly reconfigured for mushroom growing. Laurence Laboutière (her moniker is "Laurence Champignon") cultivates ten varieties, including the famous gilled pleurotus, the "Pomponnette de Montsoreau," which is just as good eaten raw and which she sells at the Sunday food market, not far from a very popular rummage sale that takes place every second Sunday of the month. Laurence also likes to cook the mushrooms at her friend Nicole's, who lives in one of the village's twenty-one troglodyte dwellings (*troglos*, as they like to say here)—comfortable caves with all modern conveniences.

Officially recognized as one of the "Most Beautiful Villages of France," granted the status of "Flowered Village," and now on UNESCO's World Heritage list, this delightful place on the banks of the Loire, nestled in the heart of the nature reserve of Loire-Anjou-Touraine (the visitor center, or "Maison du Parc," is here), well deserves a visit. Aside from its church of Saint-Pierre-de-Rest and its splendid panorama, Montsoreau is also known for its competitions of *boule de fort*, a ball game invented in the seventeenth century by Spanish prisoners. Governed by strict rules applied in gentle good humor, the game is played in a convivial spirit typical of Montsoreau.

published in 1846. The book takes the customary liberties with regard to historical veracity, but it tells of the star-crossed love of Diane de Méridor (her real name was Françoise de Maridor), the wife of the count of Monsoreau, and her beau, Louis de Bussy d'Amboise. The story takes place in the sixteenth century against the background of the French Wars of Religion. Twice adapted for television, in 1971 and 2009, this tear-jerker brought Montsoreau a certain celebrity and a significant increase in the number of visitors.

It was a stroke of luck for the village. Montsoreau is equally fortunate in having some excellent building material—the local tuffeau—practically on site. The white ashlar from which both the château and the

At Le Saut-aux-Loups, immense galleries left by the extraction of tuffeau stone have been used to grow mushrooms for over a century.

# SAINTE-SUZANNE

William the Conqueror had his beady eye on it. On several occasions between 1083 and 1087 he attempted to take the town, but it resisted, and the king left with his tail between this legs. It was the first claim to fame of this "pearl of the Mayenne," but not the last. The medieval town of Sainte-Suzanne, overlooking the valley of the Erve between Laval and Le Mans, has now been officially recognized as one of the "Most Beautiful Villages of France" and serves as a center for outdoor recreation.

In 2009, it was awarded a diploma by the "Society for the Protection of the Landscape and Aesthetics," and in November 2011 won a regional award for its floral displays. Furthermore, the castle has come top in a list of monuments that provide easy access for disabled visitors. Solidly anchored at the top of a high cliff on an isolated hill, Sainte-Suzanne occupies a strategic position in the heart of the Maine. From its rocky overhang, it benefits from a superb vista over the hills of the Coëvrons and the plain of Anjou. The defensive qualities of the site must have been appreciated by early

humans, because just a couple of miles from the castle keep stands the dolmen of the Erves, one of the best-known and most ancient megalithic monuments in the Mayenne. Recent archaeological digs have also uncovered a Celtic settlement from the sixth and fifth centuries BCE.

The fortifications that have earned Sainte-Suzanne its fame are arranged on a curious triangular plan. The perimeter can be followed via the path that leads from

*Facing page*: From an isolated hilltop above a 230-foot (70-m) cliff, the village of Sainte-Suzanne surveys the Coëvrons hills and the plain of Anjou.

*Left*: The village is full of charming lanes and houses dating back to the Middle Ages.

*Above*: Poking above the rooftops is one of the château's towers. This magnificent pile was constructed in the early seventeenth century for Guillaume Fouquet de La Varenne, who never had time to complete the vast estate he had planned.

the postern, which hugs the two steepest sides of the ramparts. Passing in front of the Tour de Guet, take the Porte de Fer, which leads to the castle's courtyard and to four lookout turrets. You then arrive at the Porte du Guichet, through which you enter the town along the main thoroughfare, the Grande Rue. Number 7 is the Maison de l'Auditoire, formerly used as a courtroom and today a museum of the town's history, which boasts the oldest piece of armor in France. Below the town hall, which occupies the site of the old market, the *grenier à sel* used to store salt—at that time an extremely valuable commodity—before it was sold on to twenty-six neighboring parishes. To open its locks required the use of three different keys, held by three different people. To the east, the seventeenth-century château and a keep built in the eleventh century complete the upper part of town.

Having fended off the English for three centuries, Sainte-Suzanne eventually fell into their hands in 1425. They occupied it for fourteen years before it was retaken by Jean de Bueil, one of the companions of Joan of Arc. In time Sainte-Suzanne passed on to Henry IV of France, to whom the town pledged its allegiance, thereby accruing numerous advantages. Fouquet de La Varenne, the first governor-general of the postal service, purchased the estate from the king's first wife, Queen Margot, in 1608, building a "manor house" here (the current château). In 1661, Louis XIV granted letters patent to the town, thereby bestowing on it the privilege of holding six annual fairs. Moreover, its prosperity was furthered by the construction of seventeen mills on the Erve, which produced paper and playing cards. Today, handicraft has made a triumphant return. Outside his workshop, each craftsman displays the image of a figure from the tarot cards, painted by a local artist, the late Jean-Claude Flornoy. To help younger inhabitants appreciate the history of the town—which also features a museum of toys and enamel plaques, including the reconstruction of a classroom from the time when pupils' fingers were stained with violet ink—guides dressed up as knights or princesses conduct special walks along the ramparts. All the villagers, conscious of the exceptional heritage in their care, regularly help out with restoration work, trowel in hand.

In 2007, Juliette and Philippe fell head over heels in love with a sorry-looking pile right in the town center. Following its restoration, they transformed it into a first-rate vacation home with the romantic name of Les Fiancés de Sainte-Suzanne. If you are tempted to stay here and explore the area, a member of the Truite Suzannaise angling club would be glad to point out the best spots along the River Erve to cast a line.

> The recipient of countless accolades, this proud and elegant town has developed a significant sense of community thanks to the determination of its inhabitants.

*Facing page*: At the foot of the château, a pathway leaves from the watchtower, skirts the castle, and then passes outside the ramparts. A stop at the Porte de Fer affords views down to the river and its watermill, or Grand Moulin.

Above: Sainte-Suzanne and its château viewed from the meadows on the banks of the River Erve.

*Right*: A painstakingly and tastefully restored medieval façade on the Rue de la Belle Étoile.

# PICARDY

Parfondeval
Gerberoy

THE ROLLING PLATEAUS and vast horizons of Picardy—the gateway to the Île-de-France—seem endless. With their scattering of hills, the neatly compartmentalized areas of the Tardenois, the Valois, and the Soissonnais are blessed with rich agricultural plains, as well as impressive forests. Around Compiègne, Chantilly, Senlis, and Villers-Cotterêts, coppices, heather moors, stands of trees, and undergrowth remind us of the great royal hunts that took place here; and it remains a wonderful place for riding. All that changes at Bray, where there are meadows separated by hedgerows, and an excellent clay soil much appreciated by potters from the Middle Ages on. To the north, in the country of Laon, Saint-Quentin, and Amiens, farms are scattered around towns and villages with Gothic bell towers. The Oise, which slices diagonally across Picardy, has been a chief axis of settlement and transportation for millennia, while the Somme and its tributaries are a favorite haunt of anglers and hikers. The latter, having molded a landscape of plains and dales, drifts into the English Channel by way of a vast estuary bordered to the south by cliffs, and to the north by sandy beaches protected by a band of pebbles. A safe stopover for migrants to and from warmer climes, this bay—now a nature reserve—offers refuge to more than three hundred species of birds. Beyond, dunes skirt the beaches of the Marquenterre. Ruled at times by the French, the Burgundians, or even the English, Picardy has been a hostage to the fluctuating fortunes of others, though this has not prevented it from constructing a strong regional identity based around its remarkable dialect.

*Facing page*: A wheat field on the Chemin des Dames in the Aisne. Along with beet and potato, wheat is one of the principal crops grown in Picardy, a major agricultural region.

*Left*: Huts on the beach at Cayeux-sur-Mer, a seaside resort on the Bay of the Somme; the castle at Pierrefonds, an immense late fourteenth-century fortress saved from ruin in the nineteenth century by Viollet-le-Duc; a brick-built house typical of the area round Amiens.

# GERBEROY

O n the borders between Normandy and Picardy, in the center of a triangle marked out by Beauvais, Rouen, and Amiens, Gerberoy is a haven of peace and quiet: no stores, no school. It is isolated, but certainly not lonely. Awash with climbing roses, the village spreads out from two cobbled streets bordered by seventeenth- and eighteenth-century houses made of cob and half-timbering, with pink brick studwork or flint infill, as spick and span as the day they were built. Restored, revamped, beautified by its hundred inhabitants, the village owes its revival to the painter Henri Le Sidaner (1862–1939). In midsummer 1900, on the advice of a friend, the ceramist Auguste Delaherche, the artist set up his easel in the Beauvais, painting the local scenery and stumbling across this ancient fortified town while taking a walk. Beguiled, he returned to spend the next summer there. "I was astonished to find myself in a little old town, rather sleepy, yet infused with the charm of its past," he wrote, discreetly passing over the sorry state of his discovery at the time. At the epicenter of many Franco-English conflicts, the site was besieged, overrun, and retaken countless times between 1079 and 1437; it was even set ablaze on three occasions, in 1611, 1651, and 1673. Despite its small size, the king of France, Philip Augustus, granted it town status in 1202. Nonetheless, it bears the wounds of hard-fought battles. Its collegiate church of Saint-Pierre, erected in 1015 but burned down in 1419, was rebuilt between 1451 and 1468; it flanks the buttress of a keep that

Close to the town hall, the communal well, 230 feet (70 m) deep and protected by a tiled wellhead, was restored by the inhabitants, like many other buildings in Gerberoy.

disappeared long ago. Hardly had Le Sidaner arrived in the house he had bought than the artist was placing his creative talents at the disposal of the entire village—its houses, lanes, and public spaces. For his own pleasure, he restored the ruins of the old fortress, which had been dismantled at the end of the sixteenth century, turning it into a splendid garden influenced by his journeys to England and Italy. It remains visible from the tree-shaded promenade on the ramparts. Gerberoy inspired a hundred or so canvases that emanate a *douceur de vivre* and a consoling sense that time has stopped. It is

a sentiment that the Picarde Élodie Gossuin, one time Miss France and Miss Europe, shares: "It is a village that feels totally at one," she declares; "I would love to live here."

Benoît Guilloux has done just that. Six years ago, together with wife and children, he returned to live in Gerberoy, where he grew up. Once a military man, he has converted his family house, a modest eighteenth-century manor, into a guesthouse. His old stables now house the Jardin du Vidamé restaurant, which serves quiches, organic soups, Petit Gerberoy (a fromage frais

A ravishing village that owes much to the splendid blooms on its rose bushes, wisterias, and lilacs, as well as to its medieval architecture. Simply enchanting!

with candied rose petals), and home-baked tarts and cakes. The rooms in the main block offer unspoilt views of the collegiate church: a fine edifice with a wooden-vaulted nave, beautiful choir stalls with carved miseri-cords, and two altarpieces of the seventeenth century. Benoît is only too pleased to accompany visitors on a tour around the village, taking in the house of Henry IV, where the sovereign is supposed to have had a wound dressed in 1591. A stone's throw from the Maison Bleue, which now houses a ceramics workshop, the cobbled street leads to the old castle gate. The first floor of the brick-built town hall shelters a market hall, while on the second floor, in the former "room of seigniorial jus-tice," is a museum containing local records. Right next to the town hall is a well some 230 feet (70 m) deep—an invaluable asset in the event of a siege.

Not only is Gerberoy officially listed as one of the "Most Beautiful Villages of France," it was also classi-fied as a "Town of Roses" in 1928. Every third Sunday in June it organizes a rose festival; on the first and second Sundays in July it holds an event dedicated to world music; and on the last Sunday in November is the vil-lage's foie gras market.

*Facing page*: The garden created at the beginning of the twentieth century by the painter Henri Le Sidaner. Its design exploits the uneven ground and incorporates the ruined ramparts.

*Top, left*: Now a ceramics workshop, the "Blue House" at the corner of two paved lanes dates back to 1691. A miniature jewel, with its blue-painted timbers and woodwork, it is the village's emblem.

*Top, right*: A colonnade in the old marketplace.

*Bottom*: The village is organized around two cobblestoned lanes lined with low half-timbered houses.

# PARFONDEVAL

eaceable Parfondeval lives the life of a rural village in the Thiérache to the full. Paris is just 112 miles (180 km) away, and Saint-Quentin just 47 miles (75 km), but from here they feel like the other side of the world. In Parfondeval, people take their time and listen respectfully to the sounds of nature. Parfondeval, like everywhere else in the region, particularly appreciates peace and quiet: from the Hundred Years War to World War II, this area at the crossroads of the Nord, Belgium, and the Ardennes has seen more than its fair share of conflict.

Today, the visitor can gaze over meadows with cows chewing the cud, wheat fields, and apple orchards. Against this background of greenery, Parfondeval is a place of easy living, scenic beauty, and architectural riches. At its heart lies a patch of grass and a pretty duck pond. "This is the pond where the cattle used to be watered; it's our village green. There were farms and ponds everywhere around here," explains Alain Turck, a man imbued with the village's history who fights to keep it alive. Its delightful red-brick houses, with slate roofs and fronts ornamented with diamond shapes in colorful glazed brick, form a harmonious whole.

*Facing page*: Located in a border area that has seen many battles, the fortified church of Saint-Médard features a large, square keep that elongates the nave.

*Above, left*: An adorable brick house, typical of the Thiérache, shaded by vines.

*Above, right*: A statue of the Virgin and Child in the church of Saint-Médard.

This calm rural village, with its typical regional architecture, possesses a discreet charm. At its heart is an undoubted masterpiece: the fortified church of Saint-Médard.

The houses are clustered round the fortified sixteenth-century church of Saint-Médard, forming a sort of enclosure around the ecclesiastical building, reached through a small, temple-shaped porch. Likewise built in brick, it displays a Renaissance doorway in white stone. The tower-cum-keep is flanked by two circular towers that protect the entrance, while the overhanging arcade supports a covered walkway. This was a defensive system that could be barricaded at the slightest warning, allowing the population to take refuge in a room twenty-three feet (7 m) square concealed above the vestibule. "This church was reinforced at the end of the Hundred Years War to protect the population from marauding bands that ravaged the region," explains Lucien, the local beadle and the village's living memory, as he shows us around the listed historic monument.

Parfondeval also has a Protestant church of the nineteenth century that has played its own role in local history. Four hundred years earlier, some Parfondevalois went to the plain of Meaux to work on the harvest. There they came across a Bible translated into French and the new ideas promulgated by Luther. This hailed the beginning of the Protestant Reformation in the Thiérache region. Parfondeval was split into two, with the upper town occupied by Catholics and the lower by Protestants. That is a thing of the past, however: now the two denominations get on well and both take part in village activities. Once a year, about thirty artists and art craftsmen of the Thiérache, the Nord, the Netherlands, and Belgium take over several barns placed at their disposal, while ten local producers prepare a typical lunch under two big awnings. The great majority of Parfondeval's citizens make their living from agriculture. It is easy to visit one of the dairy herds, such as that belonging to Jean-Luc Pruvot. It is a family business that he manages along with his father and son—three generations of stockbreeders under the same roof. Jean-Luc

owns about ninety dairy cows, all carefully selected. He likes to breed "stars": exceptional animals that shine in farm shows and at the Salon de l'Agriculture, where he has already won several prizes.

Parfondeval has kept its country soul and is proud of it. Lucien has turned his house at the foot of the church into a museum of old tools, of which he owns at least three thousand. He strokes the much-used blades and the handles worn smooth by hands toiling on the land. To spellbound adults and children, he explains how best to use them so as not to tire oneself out.

*Facing page*: The dark glazed-brick diaper patterns on the church porch contrast attractively with the red background.

*Above*: The spire of Saint-Médard rises above the surrounding meadows and apple trees.

*Left*: The church's timber-framed nave.

# POITOU-CHARENTES

Angles-sur-l'Anglin

Talmont-sur-Gironde

**FROM THE WEST** of the Charente to the borders of Vienne, from way out in the Deux-Sèvres to the shores of Charente-Maritime, Poitou-Charentes offers a delightful scenic kaleidoscope. Between the undulating country of the Vienne, the shadowy marshlands of the Poitevin, and the Atlantic coast, there is much to discover here. You just have to do a little walking, grab a bicycle, or encounter a Poitou ass (robust but sweet-natured) grazing in a field. Or you could board a *gabarre* and sail on the Charente, down past Jarnac and Cognac all the way to the ocean.

The best food here is drawn exclusively from the land: butter from local pastures, cheese from Chabichou, lamb from Poitou, poultry from the Sèvres valley, melons from Haut-Poitou, fish in abundance from the rivers and the sea, and Marenne oysters. There's plenty of wine, too, from the Haut-Poitou and the Thouarsais, as well as the famous Pineau de Charentes. One can take up a pilgrim's staff and explore the Romanesque wonders dotted about the St. James's Way that leads to Santiago de Compostela. Poitiers, La Rochelle, Niort, Angoulême, Châtellerault, Rochefort, Royan— all these cities proclaim their rich past in their stones, as do the towns and a. Cardinal Richelieu left his imprint on Richelieu and Brouage. Outgoing and reserved at the same time, both rural and coastal, rustic and modern, the region of Poitou-Charentes is a country of dreams. A trip to the Futuroscope multimedia theme park will transport you to another dimension—or you could just sail off to the islands of Ré or Oléron.

*Facing page*: A typical local house on the banks of the Sèvre Niortaise river, which descends to the marshland of Poitou.

*Left*: Pebbles collected from the beach decorate a door on the Île de Ré; a very old breed, the Poitou ass has an unusually long coat; the *chabichou*, a soft, cylindrical goat's-milk cheese produced in Poitou, now protected by an AOC (*appellation d'origine contrôlée*) certification.

# ANGLES-SUR-L'ANGLIN

The mayor of Angles-sur-l'Anglin, located on the borderland of Berry, Touraine, and Poitou, was elected for his managerial qualities, but also because he has green fingers. Under Bernard Tricoche's auspices, the inhabitants (known as Anglois) have gone into floral overdrive, adapting their displays to the architecture. In fact, it's something they've always done here—just a tradition reasserting itself.

The 385 Anglois adore their village. It owes its name to the tribe of the Angles, who invaded England in the fifth century. Their name subsequently became synonymous with the English, their successors, who attacked France during the Hundred Years War. Having defeated the French at Crécy in 1346, the English undertook yearly raids, with incursions as far as the Périgord and, on occasion, Angles-sur-l'Anglin. It was here that they came across the wealthy abbey of Sainte-Croix, whose church survives. There has been a fortress on the abrupt cliffs dominating the valley of Anglin at least since the eleventh century. It looks off-putting, perhaps, but when there's booty to be grabbed! In 1356, after John II of France's humiliating defeat at Poitiers, scarcely twenty-seven miles (43 km) away, the situation was

*Facing page*: The chapel of Sainte-Croix, with its splendid thirteenth-century entrance, adjoins an old abbey devastated by Protestants during the French Wars of Religion

*Above*: Located at the crossroads of three provinces and preserving much of its medieval character, the upper town of Angles-sur-l'Anglin stands proudly on its cliff top while the lower town occupies both banks of the river.

*Above*: The wheel of the old communal mill at Anglin still turns today.

*Facing page, top*: The old castle has guarded the eastern frontier of Poitou since the eleventh century.

*Facing page, bottom*: Counting stitches for the openwork embroidery known as *jours d'Angles*, which used to decorate the tablecloths in the Élysée Palace, is meticulous work.

desperate. The English had taken the king prisoner and were asking the sum of four million golden *écus* by way of ransom. Negotiations began. The fortress at Angles was defended by Guichard IV of Oyré on behalf of its lord, the bishop of Poitiers. At the demand of his captive king, he ceded to the command of the Black Prince, eldest son of the king of England, delivering up the fortress and serving him devotedly. Awarded the Order of the Garter, he became governor to the prince's sons. Now wealthy, he refurbished the castle, which became known as the Château Guichard, but in 1372 Bertrand de Guesclin seized it from the English. The Wars of Religion scarcely treated it better. The Huguenots of Coligny seized the place in 1567, but it was retaken by the Catholic League in 1591. Castle, church, abbey, and village were plundered. In the Revolution, the château was declared a public quarry, but once the timber had been removed the stone became difficult to reach, and the destruction halted. The property of the commune since 1986, it is now a peaceful tourist attraction. All its misadventures did not prevent Angles-sur-l'Anglin from enjoying considerable prosperity in the sixteenth and seventeenth centuries. Located at the intersection of three provinces, and blessed by a river, the Anglin (where the old mill still turns), it hosted markets and fairs selling local produce—especially wheat, the raw material for the *broyé du Poitou*, a large wafer traditionally broken in two by being punched in the middle. In the nineteenth century, local embroiderers consolidated the village's fame. They invented a type of openwork embroidery that they continued to make until the 1960s, supplying fabric to major couturiers, and tablecloths to the Élysée Palace and the *SS France*, an ocean liner.

Angles is now reveling in a second youth. It has kept its school. Bars and restaurants remain open year round. Tourists come in droves to explore the upper and lower town, with its old alleyways and houses, before taking refreshments in the shade of the lime trees on the main square. They arrive by car and bicycle, on the footpath, or by canoe on the River Anglin. They are also attracted by the Roc aux Sorciers, one of the country's most significant Paleolithic sites. Like Geneviève Pinçon, the conservator, and Oscar Fuentes, who oversees its visitor center, people are fascinated by this cave shelter, where people of the Magdalenian culture carved, engraved, and painted realistic human and animal figures some 15,000 years ago.

JEANINE PORTE, born into a family of embroiderers and a needlewoman herself, explains: "One has to draw the thread through before reinforcing the openwork with special stitches." Along with five friends, she belongs to an association dedicated to the promotion of the *jours d'Angles*, striving to safeguard this heritage under threat. A growing number of amateur embroiderers are learning the ropes via introductory courses held in the afternoons.

*Above*: The church of Sainte-Radegonde, known for being "at the mercy of the waters," stands in front of the Gironde estuary. Hanging almost from the ramparts, a square *carrelet* net waits to be cast.

*Facing page, left*: The elegant form of a wrought-iron door knocker.

*Facing page, right*: With their white frontages and blue shutters, the typical houses of Talmont-sur-Gironde consist of a ground floor and a more modest upper story, whose windows are directly under the roof.

*Pages 220–21*: Jutting into the estuary and surrounded by ramparts, Talmont-sur-Gironde preserves its original walled plan. Its streets and lanes are laid out at right angles.

# TALMONT-SUR-GIRONDE

Twenty minutes by car from Royan, Talmont-sur-Gironde is both a stopover and a destination in itself. Peering out of the waters, this small town girdled by ramparts offers a halt on the road to Bordeaux, just as it did for medieval pilgrims on the way to Santiago de Compostela, who would catch their breath and grab something to eat before taking up their staffs once again. But it is also a destination simply because the road stops here, at the end of a promontory. This enclosed town was ordained by Edward I of England in 1284. Jacques Chardonne, a writer from Charente, once said of the place: "Here, all is silence, illuminations of white walls and tall, dewy blooms."

Overhanging the estuary of the Gironde, it preserves the original plan of a walled hamlet. It should be explored on foot to appreciate the gentle charm of its streets and its lanes, which intersect at right angles. The village's houses, with their white frontages and blue shutters crouching behind banks of hollyhocks, consist of a ground floor and a more modest upper story, whose little windows huddle beneath the eaves. Whether or not they pass by the central square, where an age-old lime tree grows, all roads lead to Sainte-Radegonde, a church described as being "at the mercy of the waters," and the symbol of the Poitou-Charentes region. Planted firmly in front of the Gironde estuary, the church defies the waters and the weather. Built by monks from Saint-Jean-d'Angély, and pure Saintonge Romanesque in style, it was fortified at the end of the thirteenth century and still displays a good proportion of its ramparts. A small seamen's cemetery occupies a nearby cliff top, where wayside flowers grow untroubled. It possesses several cenotaphs, evidence

> Dusk on a summer's evening is the perfect time to walk through this ancient village.

of the revival of funerary art in the eighteenth century. Together, church and cemetery face out to eternity, its mystery and silence.

From the church, a little farther south, visitors can make out the white cliff of Caillaud and some pretty fishing huts on piles: the *carrelets*, whose name comes from the square nets cast by the fishermen. These spots have existed for a good hundred years. There's only one way to spend time in the huts: you have to know one of the lucky owners. Odette tells of life in these tiny houses: "No need for telephone or TV. Nothing! Nature, rest, the birds, and sun. And then the fishing: it's fishing for fun, but it's ecologically responsible, too, because when a fish is too small it's thrown back in the water."

In Talmont, everyone finds their own version of happiness. Christine runs a store in the village, but she is also a musician and a poet. "To create, one needs all this," she declares, gesturing to the scenery with a broad sweep of her arm. "I owe every word I write to Talmont, to this village, just as it is—to nature, which is everywhere, and to the vineyards not far off. Life is made to be loved, on a foggy day or in the pale light of morning. Alone, we make the most of our time, so we must live each moment fully." At the end of the day, a *yole*, the traditional skiff used by the estuary's fishers, returns to port with Tutu, the fisherman everyone knows, aboard. The fishing was good, and the day's catch is sold at the market on the quayside.

There's no better way to end the day than taking a stroll along the seafront. Yannick savors this great gulp of fresh air: "I sometimes find myself all alone before a splendid sunset. I reckon I'm incredibly lucky, and for nothing on earth would I live anywhere else."

The white-painted houses in this peaceful lane are adorned with stands of hollyhocks.

*Top*: The church of Sainte-Radegonde and the seamen's cemetery.

*Bottom, left*: A corbel carved into the head of a fierce-looking animal looks out from beneath the church roof.

*Bottom, right*: *Carrelet* nets are silhouetted against the sea at dusk.

# PROVENCE-ALPES-CÔTE D'AZUR

Moustiers-Sainte-Marie
Les Baux-de-Provence

THE PROVENCE-ALPES-CÔTE D'AZUR region is still a fashion Eldorado for the sun-lovers and jetsetters who flock there in summer. They roast on the beaches, frolic in its waters, stay up all night, and dream of it all year long. Cannes, with its film festival and red carpet, signals the beginning of the "season." It is a fun, ephemeral international melting pot that spills out into a region where sunshine and sea reign supreme. Backing on to the Prealps, washed by the Mediterranean sea, and bordered by the legendary Rhône, Provence-Alpes-Côte d'Azur has been a land "blessed by the gods" since remotest antiquity. It has long been a destination where people, young and less young alike, come to watch the world go by, and forms a densely populated strip that extends from the valleys of the Rhône and the Durance to Italy.

The dynamism of the region is ensured by Marseille, a port turned toward Africa and the Middle East, and the European Capital of Culture for 2013, and Nice, the second most populated city. For half a century Avignon has acted as a magnet to theatergoers, and with its famous "Pont," its popes, and their palace forms an ideal venue. Arles, with its bullring and its statue of the Provençal poet Frédéric Mistral, is heavy with the scents of the South. Aix-en-Provence, where René of Anjou ended his days and where Cézanne was born, owes its reputation to its shaded Cours Mirabeau and its café terraces. At the foot of Mont Faron, Toulon—the largest French naval port—is a center of international research. Inland, between Cavaillon and Manosque, stretches the Lubéron. The Lourmarin valley, a favorite of Albert Camus, slices it in two. To the west, its uplands rub up against those of the Alpilles. To the east, splendid villages on the hillsides attract painters, writers, and artists.

*Facing page*: A field of lavandin, a hybrid between two types of lavender, on the Valensole plateau. Ranging from green to mauve, such fields owe their beauty to the men who dig and plant the furrows.

*Left*: A traditional sailboat in the port of Saint-Tropez; the Italian-influenced façade of a substantial townhouse in Nice; Camargue horses gallop near Saintes-Marie-de-la-Mer.

# LES BAUX-DE-PROVENCE

In the heart of the regional nature reserve of the Alpilles, Les Baux-de-Provence possesses a charm and a fragrance that makes it stand out from every other village in the region. As author André Suarès wrote to the sculptor Antoine Bourdelle: "I know of no place more admirable than Les Baux. It is a landscape that cuts us off from everything offensive." High on a rocky outcrop and overlooked by an imposing stronghold, Les Baux is a stone citadel reigning over a landscape of vineyards and olive groves, and kissed by the sun three hundred days per year. Officially recognized for its beauty and good taste, as well as being one of the "Most Beautiful Villages of France," Les Baux has earned a screed of titles.

This eyrie had already been sealed off behind a ring of fortifications in the eleventh century. In the thirteenth century, to demonstrate the might of their lineage, Hugues and Barral des Baux, the local lords, added a keep and a few dwellings. At the end of the Middle Ages, however, on the death of Alix, the last princess of Les Baux, the medieval château, which had so often been used against central authority, was seized by Louis III, king of Sicily and count of Provence. The borough and its lands became part of the royal domain when Provence was annexed to the French crown by Louis XI, who ordered the fortress to be dismantled in 1483. The magnanimous monarch, however, permitted Les Baux to keep its customs, franchises, and prerogatives. In 1642, Louis XIII bestowed the overlordship of Les Baux on Hercule Grimaldi, who handed down the title of "marquis of Les Baux" to his descendants, including Prince Albert II of Monaco, the current incumbent.

If Les Baux numbered about three thousand inhabitants in the thirteenth century, by the late nineteenth this had plummeted to a mere four hundred. Today,

*Facing page*: On a square shaded by cypress trees at the top of the cliff, the chapel of the Pénitents Blancs, built in the seventeenth century by members of the brotherhood, and the Romanesque church of Saint-Vincent both look down on the delightful Vallon de la Fontaine.

*Left*: The ruined city wall offers a dazzling panorama over the plain of Tarascon, toward Arles and the Camargue.

*Pages 228–29*: Just below the citadel is the "hellish" Val d'Enfer, dug out of the rock by erosion.

*Above, top left*: Craftsmen called *santonniers* still make these typical clay figurines for Christmas cribs. A museum in the old guardhouse at the Eyguières gate displays several collections of *santons*.

*Above, bottom left*: A Renaissance doorway at the Hôtel Jean-de-Brion. The house was restored by Louis Jou, a publisher and engraver, whose workshop and well-stocked library are now open to the public.

*Above, right*: Relaxing to music in the streets of Les Baux.

*Facing page*: *Post Tenebras Lux* ("after darkness comes light"): a Calvinist motto engraved on a Renaissance window frame. This is the only remaining part of a sizable sixteenth-century house that was probably employed for Protestant services.

The stone fortress is a veritable open-air museum. I also appreciate the panorama and its flavors of Provence.

there are no more than nineteen residents in the historic quarter. Olive producer Jean-Benoît Hugues knows them all. He likes to linger on the Place Louis Jou, on the terrace of the Relais de la Porte Eyguières, run by Mme Chabanier, whose family has lived here for four centuries.

In the aftermath of World War II, Les Baux-de-Provence embarked on a new career as a tourist attraction and cultural center. In 1947, Raymond Thuillier opened the celebrated Oustau de Baumanière, where the great and the good flocked like bees around a honeypot: Queen Elizabeth, Brad Pitt and Angelina Jolie, Johnny Depp, writer André Malraux (who, in 1966, placed the whole commune under the protection of the Ministry of Culture and the Environment), Bono. At the present time, the hotel is managed by Jean-André Charial, the founder's grandson. The ovens are manned by Sylvestre Wahid, a remarkable chef born in Pakistan.

Many people visiting the theater festival in Avignon, just nineteen miles (30 km) away, spend at least a day in Les Baux, wandering the medieval lanes, and slowly exploring the twenty-two listed monuments and other treasures the village conceals. Among these are the church of Saint-Vincent, which displays both Romanesque and Renaissance elements, and beautiful stained-glass windows by Max Ingrand; a Renaissance window frame inscribed *Post Tenebras Lux* ("after darkness comes light"), a moving testament

to Huguenot influence; sixteenth- and seventeenth-century mansions, now converted into art galleries and museums; the Musée Yves Brayer; a collection of *santons* (Christmas figures); and the town hall that occupies the Hôtel de Manville. Some forty-six feet (14 m) high, the vast Carrières de Lumières provide a backdrop for spectacular multimedia shows. An exploration of the quarry can be followed by a walk through the Val d'Enfer: situated below the village, this "Vale of Hell" presents a succession of bizarre and fantastical rock formations. Tradition has it that this scenery provided Dante with the inspiration for his *Inferno*. Cocteau shot his film *The Testament of Orpheus* here. Mireille, the heroine of Frédéric Mistral's poem written in Occitan, bears her wounded lover, Vincent, to this very spot. One of the caverns here, which opens onto a narrow gully, is supposedly inhabited by a witch who concocts much vaunted healing potions. With so much to offer, it should come as no surprise to learn that Les Baux-de-Provence caters for more than one-and-a-half million visitors each year.

# MOUSTIERS-SAINTE-MARIE

In the Alpes de Haute-Provence, the houses of Moustiers-Sainte-Marie are arranged in rows against an azure sky. Leaning against the cliff, and listed as one of the "Most Beautiful Villages of France," this village is located at the intersection between the great Verdon Gorge and the lavender route that crosses the plateau of Valensole. At the heart of the Verdon nature reserve and hard by the artificial Lac de Sainte-Croix, made in 1974, its narrow lanes alternate with arched passages, little squares, wash-houses, fountains, and humpbacked bridges. Ancient dwellings with corbels and tiled roofs rub shoulders with grand residences of the eighteenth century, entered through splendid wooden doors. "Nowhere else do you have that combination of the green gorges of the Verdon, nature, lavender, and stone," enthuses Alain Ducasse, one of the world's most celebrated chefs, who was struck with admiration for "this place blessed by the Gods ... long ago."

Moustiers is best contemplated from the chapel of Notre-Dame-de-Beauvoir. It is reached via a staircase of 262 steps, which includes the Stations of the Cross. In the Middle Ages it was known as a *sanctuaire à répit*, a holy place dedicated to the Virgin whose intercession was necessary for a particular miracle to take place. According to popular belief among the Catholics of Provence, prayers might allow still-born children to return to life—for a brief moment only—in order to be baptized. The child could thus enter paradise, from which it would otherwise be barred.

Although acknowledged as one of the "Most Beautiful Villages of France," Moustiers does not owe its

worldwide reputation to its scenery but to its faience. Much appreciated by the French nobility in the seventeenth and eighteenth centuries, these lavish pieces are today highly regarded by antiques dealers and collectors. Tradition states that the technique was introduced by a monk returning from Italy, where he had learned the secret of the fine milk-white enamel that, together with the so-called "Moustiers" blue, makes these ceramics so famous. In any event, faience production could never have thrived here without the clay, water, and wood local potters found on the spot. At the beginning of the nineteenth century, sales suffered owing to the appearance of Limoges porcelain and the arrival of English china. The last kiln flickered out in 1874, only to be relit in 1927. At the present time, about fifteen potters work in the village. Christine is the daughter of one, and now a *faïencière* herself: "I often tell people I was born in a pot, here, in the workshop, as

*Facing page*: At the gateway to the Verdon Gorge, the houses of Moustiers-Sainte-Marie are arranged like an amphitheater, with views over the plateau of Valensole.

*Above, left*: The doorway to the chapel of Notre-Dame-de-Beauvoir, which is reached via a staircase of 262 steps.

*Above, right*: Forming a veritable labyrinth, shady, narrow lanes wind their way among the ancient houses.

was my sister. We grew up here. It was self-evident I'd join the business," she admits, pointing out her graceful, hand-painted decoration. Stamping, turning, enameling, painting freehand—Franck Scherer, master potter at the Atelier du Soleil, explains each time-honored step in the exacting process.

Every year, thousands of visitors leave the region with a plate or a dish, a pot or a soup tureen. But they also depart with the unforgettable image of a star that, for centuries, has hung from a chain 443 feet (135 m) long suspended between two rocky outcrops. This is the emblem of the village. Its origin remains a mystery. Legend tells of a crusader knight from Blacas taken prisoner by the Saracens. If ever he regained his freedom, he vowed, he would hang a star from a chain near the chapel of Notre-Dame-de-Beauvoir. Once back in Moustiers, he did as he promised. Skeptical, the inhabitants of Moustiers concede: "It is not known exactly why it hangs there. It falls off about twice a century. It's so important that, whenever it comes down, there's a whole ceremony to replace it. When it's not there, we feel naked, something's missing."

Is it this emblem that inspires Marie-Ange, who bakes delicious biscuits in the shape of a star? "I work with as much local produce as possible—lavender, almonds from the plateau, honey, fresh eggs," she explains. This is the sort of cuisine that delights Alain Ducasse: "The world outside does not yet hold much sway over Moustiers. That's its advantage and its difference."

This is an animated, thriving village, whose craft traditions have been revived. And its location, near the Lac de Sainte-Croix, at the foot of the Verdon Gorge, is spectacular.

*Facing page*: Moustiers, hugging a rocky escarpment below a star suspended 820 feet (250 m) above the abyss, has often been compared to a crib.

*Above, left*: By taking tiny lanes and narrow staircases, the visitor will eventually reach the church square at the village's heart.

*Above, top right*: A painted storefront in Moustiers.

*Above, bottom right*: Metal-oxide paints for decorating earthenware. The color depends on the active ingredient: copper for green, iron for yellow, manganese for brown and black, and cobalt for blue.

# RHÔNE-ALPES

Yvoire

Pérouges

ENGORGED BY ITS MANY TRIBUTARIES, the Rhône forms a kind of backbone for the eight departments of the Rhône-Alpes region, unifying it to some degree. The razor-tipped Alps, the Jura with its blunter peaks, and the gentle Massif Central occupy three-quarters of the territory, resulting in immensely varied scenery and plentiful places to ski. The Winter Olympics have been held here on no fewer than three occasions: in Chamonix in 1924, Grenoble in 1968, and Albertville in 1992. In summer, lakes and pools, in particular in the Dauphiné and Savoy, play an important role in regulating the water supply to the cities and countryside, as well as attracting anglers and ramblers. The torrents and rivers around Annecy, in Isère, the Tarentaise, and the Vercors, offer ideal opportunities for rafting and canyoneering.

The Saône joins the Rhône at Lyon. Occurring at the heart of a large metropolitan city, their confluence has spawned two thousand years of dynamic development immortalized in masonry. Awarded UNESCO World Heritage status in 1988, the old city of Lyon boasts one of the largest ensembles of Renaissance architecture in Europe. The city is especially renowned for its gastronomy, concocted over the centuries by the legendary "mothers" of Lyon, and helped down by the wines of the Beaujolais. It was here that the Lumière brothers invented the cinematograph. The puppet Guignol (a sort of "Punch"), dreamed up by a *canut* (silk-worker) and spare-time tooth-puller, was born here. The Rhône-Alpes has five national theaters and as many performing arts centers, museums, festivals (jazz at Vienne, humor at Chamrousse), and a biennial of dance in Lyon and of design in Saint-Étienne, both internationally recognized. However, it remains very much attached to its regular sequence of traditional secular and religious festivals.

*Facing page*: At the heart of the Vanoise Massif at Courchevel, a Savoyard chalet enjoys views of the Grand Bec.

*Left*: Guignol, a famous string puppet created in Lyon by Laurent Mourguet in 1808; the green landscape in the Haut-Jura nature reserve; a spot of white-water rafting.

*Above*: The renowned Hostellerie du Vieux Peroges, where Bill Clinton ignored his diet to eat a Pérouges *galette*.

*Facing page, left*: The cobbled Rue du Prince connects the church square and the Porte d'En-Haut to the old marketplace.

*Facing page, right*: The fifteenth-century fortress church of Sainte-Marie-Madeleine towers over the village.

# PÉROUGES

D
o you know how to walk the Pérouges walk, a place where it's done like nowhere else? As soon as you enter the intact Porte d'En-Haut, you have to watch your step since you're walking on *têtes de chat*. These "cat's heads" are pebbles from the plain of the Ain river that have been used as cobbles since the Middle Ages. Time loses its sting in Pérouges: it may be just twenty-nine miles (46 km) from Lyon, but the town remains medieval, with its fortress-cum-church close to the gate, its Promenade des Terreaux that follows the layout of the old moat, the Rue des Princes and Rue des Rondes, and the old marketplace shaded by a lime tree planted for the bicentenary of the Revolution. This is the home of the Maison du Petit-Saint-Georges and the Hostellerie. Farther off, the watchtower in the Maison des Princes de Savoie offers splendid views over the

village's surroundings. Every street is adorned with glorious and highly distinctive half-timbered front-ages. The Rue des Contreforts contains the Maison des Dîmes (where the tithe was collected) and the Maison du Pressoir. Elsewhere, the visitor will find the Maison Thibaut, the house of the sergeant of justice, and the old salt store. The atmosphere is such that you half expect to come across authentic monks, lawyers, nobles, bour-geoisie, or peasants, in chainmail or surcoats, at every turn. Unsurprisingly, a number of directors have chosen to use Pérouges as a film set.

One of the "Most Beautiful Villages of France," Pérouges owes its name to the Italian city of Perugia (Pérouse in French), whence hailed its founders. They established their settlement on a well-defended hill on the fringes of the Dombes plateau, dominating the Ain plain and on the crossroads of major trade routes. Now

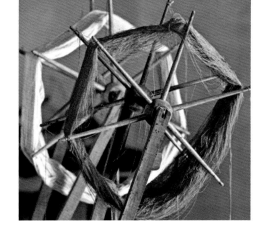

Unusually for a fortified village, Pérouges has no castle. Lovers of old stones will appreciate the beautifully restored houses in this perfect jewel of medieval architecture.

at the beating heart of the region, its elevated position helped safeguard it from the fevers that devastated this country of lakes and ponds before the development of effective medicines. Situated on the confines of France, Savoy, and the Dauphiné, it quickly became a strategically desirable possession for the two provinces that besieged it in turn, though in vain. By the fourteenth century, it served as a stronghold for the dukes of Savoy, who had granted it charters of franchise in the twelfth century as a reward for its fidelity. In 1601, the annexation of the Bresse and the Bugey to France made it less important as a border sentinel. It concentrated on growing hemp and flax crops, and on weaving—activities that had earned it prosperity and fame since the fifteenth century. The industrial revolution put paid to these endeavors, and the population deserted the old citadel. Much affected by its decrepit state, Édouard Herriot, the mayor of Lyon, became chair of the "Committee for the Conservation and Protection of Old Pérouges" in 1911, working wonders for its resurrection.

Since then, Pérouges has used its assets to good purpose. Craftsmen moved here, a museum showing a collection of everyday articles has been set up, and restaurants opened, including the renowned Hostellerie. Even if *poularde de Bresse* (chicken) is well represented on the menu, the great local specialty remains the *galette*, a kind of sweet tart. "At the beginning of the twentieth century, when bread was baked every Friday in the village oven, people would slip in a few *galettes*. They call for butter, butter, and butter. Sugar, sugar, and sugar. And cream, and yet more cream. But they're light. The secret lies in the baking," claims Georges, the owner of the restaurant where Bill Clinton dined during the G7 summit held in Lyon. "It was complicated because he was on a diet. We had to put together a menu without cream, butter, or alcohol. For a Bressan, that's impossible. But he saw sense and took a little cream with his *galette*."

*Facing page, top*: Little has changed in Pérouges, and climbing the stone staircase of a house in the Rue des Princes is like going back in time.

*Facing page, bottom left*: This sweet *galette* is a Pérouges specialty. The recipe requires butter and sugar. And then more butter and sugar. Baking is a delicate affair.

*Facing page, bottom right*: Hanks of wool on a spinning wheel in the Musée du Vieux Pérouges. The museum displays traditional furniture and other objects recalling life in bygone Bresse.

*Above*: The Porte d'En-Haut, the main entrance into the walled town.

# YVOIRE

On a peninsula south of Thonon, encircled by its fourteenth-century ramparts, Yvoire gazes down on Lake Geneva. On a war footing with the neighboring lords of the Dauphiné and the Genevois since 1306, Count Amadeus V of Savoy spotted the site and erected a fortress over a vacated fiefdom. Thereafter Yvoire guarded access to the lake, a role it performed with such panache that, in 1324, its inhabitants were rewarded with a franchise—that is to say, with certain freedoms and financial advantages. If the village survived the Middle Ages relatively unscathed, the Renaissance proved crueler. The French and the Genevois ravaged the town and set fire to the castle, which remained roofless for 350 years. Miraculously, however, the town's ramparts, gates, moats, and houses

have come down to us intact. The church dedicated to St. Pancras, probably constructed in the twelfth century, has been overhauled on several occasions. The current bell tower, built between 1854 and 1856, is topped by an onion dome characteristic of nineteenth-century Savoyard architecture. Its galvanized iron flashing was replaced by stainless steel in 1989. The cock and the ball on the summit are gilded with gold-leaf from the neighboring village of Excenevex, home to the last goldbeater in France.

Classified as one of the "Most Beautiful Villages of France," Yvoire overlooks the lake like a flowery balcony. Since 1959, it has won numerous prizes for its flowers and horticultural displays, both of which have made it a highly popular tourist destination. A million visitors come here each year, winter included, when the wind makes the stones ring and a white frost coats the banks of the lake. Twenty or so craftsmen, including a basketmaker (the only one in Haute-Savoie), are on hand to demonstrate their skill and answer questions.

At the heart of the town is a glorious château restored at the beginning of the twentieth century by the Bouvier d'Yvoire, a noble Savoyard family who have owned it since the seventeenth century. It cannot be visited, but twenty-five years ago its current owners, Yves and Anne-Monique d'Yvoire, who live there year round, planted the Jardin des Cinq Sens (the "Garden of the Five Senses"). "This garden was no longer in use. My grandfather's old gardener had passed away, and we didn't know what to do with it. My wife and I had the idea of overhauling it and opening it to the public,"

*Facing page*: The church of Saint-Pancrace, with its unusual nineteenth-century bell tower, looks down over Lake Geneva.

*Left*: A basket maker surrounded by various wares outside his workshop.

*Pages 244–45*: This château, dating from the fourteenth century, still belongs to the Yvoire family. In the castle's grounds they have created the "Garden of the Five Senses."

*Above and top right*: In 2002, Yvoire won an international trophy for its landscape design and floral displays.

*Bottom, right*: The landing stage on the shores of Lake Geneva, where the paddleboat *Le Savoie* ferries visitors across the lake.

*Facing page*: Established twenty-five years ago, the "Garden of the Five Senses" features some 1,300 species of plants. Some flowers are worth tasting, while others are remarkable for their unusual odors.

Yves explains. "Of course," adds his wife, "the parking lot had to be planned, but also 1,300 species of seedlings.... Some flowers can be nibbled, while others have a surprising fragrance. Some are nice to stroke, others are as soft as a cuddly toy." For four years, head gardener Mathieu Constant has looked after "this atypical garden containing the entire gamut of the gardener's trade." He derives immense pleasure from explaining to visitors how to tend the flowers and plants. "I encourage them to use their five senses. Here, you should feel free to touch the flowers and plants, all of which are labeled."

Lake Geneva is the dominating presence at Yvoire. After a visit around the garden, a walk along the lakeshore is highly recommend for its superb panorama of the surrounding peaks. To appreciate the landscape further, the visitor can also take a trip aboard a solar-powered shuttle that glides over the water in total silence. Of course, you shouldn't neglect the many local restaurants, where you can enjoy pan-fried fish from the lake served with cream sauce or lemon.

This village has everything. It's like a picture postcard, although far from clichéd. A magical place, it is well worth discovering.

# VISITING AND EXPLORING FURTHER

## ALSACE

### EGUISHEIM

**Tourist office**
www.ot-eguisheim.fr
Tel.: + 33 (0)3 89 23 40 33

**Les Amis des Cigognes**
This stork sanctuary is to the west,
on the fringes of the medieval walled
town and very near the campsite.
10a Rue Pasteur
68420 Eguisheim
Tel.: + 33 (0)3 89 23 18 71

**Syndicat Viticole d'Eguisheim**
The wine collective at Eguisheim
organizes events to promote
the wines of Alsace.
Contact: Tourist office

### RIQUEWIHR

**Official website**
www.riquewihr.fr

**Tourist office of the Ribeauville
and Riquewihr region**
www.ribeauville-riquewihr.com
Tel.: + 33 (0)3 89 73 23 23

**Cave de Hugel et Fils**
A wine cellar containing the oldest
working cask in the world.
3 Rue de la Première-Armée
68340 Riquewihr
info@hugel.com
www.hugel.fr
Tel.: + 33 (0)3 89 47 92 15
Visits by appointment only:
contact the owners.

**Tourist train**
SAAT
4 Rue Saint-Morand
68150 Ribeauville
info@petit-train.com
www.petit-train.com
Tel.: + 33 (0)3 89 73 74 24
Fax: + 33 (0)3 89 73 32 94

## AQUITAINE

### BEYNAC-ET-CAZENAC

**Tourist office of the Périgord Noir**
www.cc-perigord-noir.fr
Tel.: + 33 (0)5 53 31 45 45

**Viewpoint**
From the castle of Beynac over the
three castles of the "golden triangle":
Marqueyssac, Feyrac, and Castelnaud.

**Château de Beynac**
www.beynac-en-perigord.com/fr/le-
chateau.html
Tel.: + 33 (0)5 53 29 50 40

### ESPELETTE

**Official website**
www.espelette.fr
Tel.: + 33 (0)5 59 93 95 02

**Church of Saint-Étienne**
Looking like a fortress, with its thick
walls and buttresses, the porch-cum-
bell tower was erected in 1627, with
the main range dating from earlier.
A large eighteenth-century painting
above the high altar represents the
stoning of the dedicatee, St. Stephen.

**Syndicat des Producteurs de Piment**
(union of pepper producers)
Rue Principale
64250 Espelette
www.pimentdespelette.com
Tel.: + 33 (0)5 59 93 88 86
Fax: + 33 (0)5 59 93 88 92
Free entry

**Rafting, canoeing, and kayaking
on the River Nive**
Maison Lasterka
www.nature-riviere.fr
Tel.: + 33 (0)5 59 93 95 02
Cell: + 33 (0)6 19 14 27 53

**Astoklok: donkey trekking**
Ferme Belazkabieta
Belazkabietako bidea
64250 Espelette
www.astoklok.com
Tel.: + 33 (0)5 59 52 98 02
Cell: + 33 (0)6 08 78 31 96
Open all year round
Booking required

**Moonlight ramble**
Belazkabieta
64250 Espelette
www.espelette.fr
Tel.: + 33 (0)5 59 93 95 02
April to late October
Booking required

**Espelette pepper "workshop"**
Chemin de l'Église
64250 Espelette
www.atelierdupiment.com
Tel.: + 33 (0)5 59 93 90 21
Free entry

## AUVERGNE

### BLESLE

**Tourist office**
www.tourismeblesle.fr
Tel.: + 33 (0)4 71 76 26 90

**Church of Saint-Pierre**
The Romanesque church of Saint-Pierre
in Blesle was classed as a historic
monument in 1907.
Open every day from 10 a.m. to 7 p.m.
No visits during services

**Musée de la Coiffe** (traditional
headdress museum)
43450 Blesle
Tel.: + 33 (0)4 71 76 27 08;
+ 33 (0)4 71 76 20 75 (out of season)

**Trekking**
Blesle offers seventeen short rambles,
with some paths suitable for mountain
bikes; three discovery trails, two
in Blesle and one to Léotoing;
two circuits specially designed for
mountain bikes; and two car routes,
each lasting half a day.
www.tourismeblesle.fr/randonnees-
blesle-haute-loire_fr.html

### SALERS

**Tourist office**
www.salers-tourisme.fr/fr/index.aspx
Tel.: + 33 (0)4 71 40 58 08

**Hot-air balloon trips**
Alain Pirot
www.salers-montgolfiere.fr
Tel.: + 33 (0)4 71 40 77 26
Fax: + 33 (0)4 71 40 77 26
Cell: + 33 (0)6 60 96 07 73

**Visits to a Salers stockbreeder**
www.salers-tourisme.fr/fr/visiter-
fermes-pays-de-salers.aspx

**Carré d'Étoiles**
Stargazing vacations in original, cube-
shaped accommodation.
La Chaux de Revel
15140 Saint-Martin-Valmeroux
www.domainedelachauxderevel.com
Tel.: + 33 (0)4 71 40 68 10
Cell: + 33 (0)6 71 61 94 47

# BASSE-NORMANDIE

## BARFLEUR

**Official website**
www.ville-barfleur.fr/accueil.html

**Maison Paul Signac** (artist's home)
Rue Saint-Nicolas
50760 Barfleur
Open all year round
Free entry

**Pottery at Barfleur**
Rue du Vast le Cadran
50760 Barfleur
Tel.: + 33 (0)2 33 71 15 92

**Odile's marinated mackerel**
Café de France
12 Quai Henri Chardon
50760 Barfleur
Tel.: + 33 (0)2 33 54 00 38

## LA PERRIÈRE

**Orne tourist office**
www.ornetourisme.com/visites-villes-
villages/la-perriere_952.html
Tel.: + 33 (0)2 33 28 88 71

**Logis de l'Évêque**
An imposing twelfth-century house next
door to the tower, formerly part of the
estate and once used as a dungeon.
61360 La Perrière
Tel.: + 33 (0)2 33 73 35 49
Fax: + 33 (0)2 33 73 35 49

**Forest of Bellême**
www.parc-naturel-perche.fr/territoire-
belleme.asp

**La Maison d'Horbé**
A tearoom, bistro, and antiques store.
La Grande Place
61360 La Perrière
www.lamaisondhorbe.com
Tel.: + 33 (0)2 33 73 18 41
Cell: + 33 (0)6 79 83 17 96

**Art market**
Held every year in May.

# BURGUNDY

## FLAVIGNY-SUR-OZERAIN

**Official website**
www.mairie-flavignysurozerain.fr
Tel.: + 33 (0)3 80 96 21 73

**Anis de l'Abbaye de Flavigny**
(Flavigny aniseed candies)
www.anis-flavigny.com
Tel.: + 33 (0)3 80 96 20 88

**Benedictine Abbey of Saint-Pierre**
Place de l'Église
21150 Flavigny-sur-Ozerain

**La Maison des Arts Textiles
et du Design** (textile art and
design museum)
www.algranate.com
Tel.: + 33 (0)3 80 96 20 40
Cell: + 33 (0)6 80 30 98 82
or + 33 (0)6 08 83 93 82

**La Grange aux Femmes**
This restaurant located in a converted
barn serves local farm produce.
Place de l'Église
21150 Flavigny-sur-Ozerain
Tel.: + 33 (0)3 80 96 20 62
Fax: + 33 (0)3 80 96 20 62

**Winery of the Flavigny-Alésia
vineyards**
Pont Laizan
21150 Flavigny-sur-Ozerain
www.vignoble-flavigny.com
Tel.: + 33 (0)3 80 96 25 63
Fax: + 33 (0)3 80 96 25 83

## VÉZELAY

**Tourist office**
12 Rue Saint-Étienne
89450 Vézelay
www.vezelaytourisme.com
Tel.: + 33 (0)3 86 33 23 69

**Secretariat for the Basilica
of Sainte-Marie-Madeleine**
89450 Vézelay
www.jerusalem.cef.fr/monastiques/
ou-nous-trouver/vezelay-sainte-marie-
madeleine/horaires-des-offices
Tel.: + 33 (0)3 86 33 39 50

**L'Espérance**
The hotel and gastronomic restaurant
run by chef Marc Meneau.
22 Grande Rue
89450 Saint-Père
www.marc-meneau-esperance.com
Tel.: + 33 (0)3 86 33 39 10

# BRITTANY

## LOCRONAN

**Tourist office of Quimper Cornouaille
at Locronan**
www.locronan-tourisme.com
Tel.: + 33 (0)2 98 91 70 14

**Le Guillou**
Bakery and patisserie specializing in
*kouign amann* and other Breton cakes.
Place de l'Église
29180 Locronan
www.kouignamann-locronan.fr
Tel.: + 33 (0)2 98 91 70 04

**Ti Bihan** (weavers)
Atelier Le Bihan / Le Hir (weaving
workshop)
Rue du Four
29180 Locronan

Store and weaving workshop
run by Hervé Le Bihan
Place de l'Église
29180 Locronan
www.tibihan-locronan.com
Tel.: + 33 (0)2 98 91 83 78

## SAINT-SULIAC

**Official website**
www.saint-suliac.fr
Tel.: + 33 (0)2 99 58 41 22

**The Châble menhir**
Châble, on the Mont Garrot
Route de Châteauneuf (private property)
35430 Saint-Suliac

**Sailing school**
Nautical Center of Rennes/
Rance Saint-Suliac
www.nautisme-saint-suliac.com/
2012-12-04-09-31-06/2012-12-04-
12-41-21.html
Tel.: + 33 (0)2 99 58 48 80

# CENTRE

## APREMONT-SUR-ALLIER

**Official website**
www.apremont-sur-allier.com
Tel.: + 33 (0)2 48 74 25 60

**Parc Floral** (public gardens)
Le Bourg
18150 Apremont-sur-Allier
Tel.: + 33 (0)2 48 77 55 00 or 55 06

**Musée des Calèches**
(museum of carriages)
Départementale 45
18150 Apremont-sur-Allier
Tel.: + 33 (0)2 48 80 40 17
Fax: + 33 (0)2 48 80 40 17

## LAVARDIN

**Official website**
www.lavardin.net

*Chouine* (card game) World
Championships
Held on the first Sunday in March.

**Château of Lavardin**
41800 Lavardin
Tel.: + 33 (0)2 54 85 23 30
www.lavardin.net
www.otsi-montoire.fr

**Promenade du Poète**
A walk along the Loir dedicated
to the Renaissance poet Ronsard,
and a great favorite with painters
and photographers. Look out for
the former village washhouse.

**Painters' Day**
Held every Ascension Day.
www.coeurvaldeloire.com/
manifestation41/detail.asp
?idoi=FMACEN0410005814&
type=agenda-prio

# CHAMPAGNE-ARDENNES

## ESSOYES

**Tourist office**
www.ot-essoyes.fr
Tel.: + 33 (0)3 25 29 21 27

**Guided tours with Bernard Pharisien**
Tourist office of Essoyes and the
surrounding area
L'Espace des Renoir
9 Place de la Mairie
10360 Essoyes
Tel.: + 33 (0)3 25 29 21 27

**L'Espace des Renoir** (exhibition space)
9 Place de la Mairie
10360 Essoyes
www.renoir-essoyes.fr
Tel.: + 33 (0)3 25 29 10 94

**La Roseraie** (guesthouse)
Marie-Claude Dufourneaud
and Pierre Menou
6 Quai de l'Ource
10360 Essoyes
www.laroseraie-en-champagne.com
Tel.: + 33 (0)3 25 38 60 24
Cell: + 33 (0)6 80 10 62 56

## SAINT-AMAND-SUR-FION

**Information**
Monique Fuinel
monique.fuinel@wanadoo.fr
Tel.: + 33 (0)3 26 73 94 55

**Official website**
www.stamandsurfion.asso.
fr.pagesperso-orange.fr/geographie.htm

**Walking trails**
www.stamandsurfion.asso.
fr.pagesperso-orange.fr/tourisme.htm

**Musée des Voitures Hippomobiles**
(museum of horse-drawn vehicles)
51300 Saint-Amand-sur-Fion
Tel.: + 33 (0)3 26 73 94 55

# CORSICA

## CORBARA

**Official website**
www.corbara.fr

**Île Rousse tourist office**
www.ot-ile-rousse.fr
Tel.: + 33 (0)4 95 60 04 35

**Monastery of Saint-Dominique**
Congregation of St. John
www.stjean-corbara.com
Tel.: + 33 (0)4 95 60 06 73
Fax: + 33 (0)4 95 60 09 08

**Musée Guy Savelli**
The guided tour of this museum
of the history of Corsica by the owner
himself is a must.
Place de l'Église
20256 Corbara
Tel.: + 33 (0)4 95 60 06 65
Free entry

**Collegiate church of A Nunziata**
Casa Vecchielle
20256 Corbara
www.corbara.fr
Tel.: + 33 (0)4 95 63 06 50
Fax: + 33 (0)4 95 60 00 99

## PIANA

**Tourist office**
www.otpiana.com
www.piana.fr
Tel.: + 33 (0)9 66 92 84 42

**Boat trips around the coves**
www.otpiana.com/page.
php?id=92&pos=7&reset

**Chez Angelo** (butcher)
Piana
20115 Piana
Tel.: + 33 (0)4 95 27 80 93

**Le Neptune restaurant**
Hôtel Capo Rosso
Route des Calanches
20115 Piana
www.caporosso.com
Tel.: + 33 (0)4 95 27 82 40

# FRANCHE-COMTÉ

## BAUME-LES-MESSIEURS

**Official website**
www.baumelesmessieurs.fr
Tel.: + 33 (0)3 84 44 61 41
or 03 84 44 95 40 (in the tourist season)

**Abbey**
www.tourisme-hauteseille.fr/
abbaye-imperiale-de-baume.htm

**Le Dortoir des Moines**
Guest rooms in the abbey.
Jocelyne Metroz
Abbaye Saint-Pierre
39210 Baume-les-Messieurs
www.dortoir-des-moines.info/
contact.html
Tel.: + 33 (0)3 84 44 97 31

**Abbey café and restaurant**
1 Place Guillaume-de-Poupet
39210 Baume-les-Messieurs
www.restaurant-labbaye.fr
Tel.: + 33 (0)3 84 44 63 44

**The caves at Baume**
39210 Baume-les-Messieurs
www.baumelesmessieurs.fr/
?page_id=324
Tel.: + 33 (0)3 84 48 23 02 (in season);
+ 33 (0)3 84 44 61 41 (out of season)

## PESMES

**Tourist office**
www.otvaldepesmes.fr.gd/
PAGE-D-h-ACCUEIL.htm
www.pesmes.fr

**Town hall**
Tel.: + 33 (0)3 84 31 22 27

**Forges de Pesmes**
www.forgespesmes.blogspot.com
Cell: + 33 (0)6 09 92 44 29
Open all year round
Booking required

**Pesmes Loisirs**
Boating and river activities.
Chemin du Pasquier
70140 Pesmes
www.woka.fr
Tel.: + 33 (0)9 63 02 04 28

**Angling**
www.unionaappma.fr

# HAUTE-NORMANDIE

## LE BEC-HELLOUIN

**Official website**
www.lebechellouin.fr

**Tourist office**
www.tourismecantondebrionne.com
Tel.: + 33 (0)2 32 45 70 51

**Les Ateliers du Bec**
Faience workshops at the abbey.
3 Place de l'Abbé-Herluin
27800 Le Bec-Hellouin
www.abbayedubec.com
Tel.: + 33 (0)2 32 43 72 60

**Abbey**
Tel.: + 33 (0)2 32 43 72 60
Tel.: + 33 (0)2 32 43 72 62
(for accommodation)
Open every day
Information regarding retreats available
from the monks

## VEULES-LES-ROSES

**Official website**
www.veules-les-roses.fr

**Tourist office**
Tel.: + 33 (0)2 35 97 63 05

**Rambling around Veules**
www.plateaudecauxmaritime.com/
docs/331-2-veules-les-roses-circuit-
du-plus-petit-fleuve-de-france.pdf

**Watersports**
www.veules-les-roses.fr/dossiers/
cat.php?val=46

**Watercress for sale**
www.plateaudecauxmaritime.com/Les-
Cressonnieres/VEULES-LES-ROSES/
fiche-DEGNOR076FS0006V-1.html

**Trekking**
www.veules-les-roses.fr/dossiers/
dossier.php?val=58

**L'Huître de Veules**
Discover Veules oysters, available
Saturday and Sunday mornings all year
round on the beach at Veules-les-Roses.
Tel.: + 33 (0)2 35 97 29 98
Cell: + 33 (0)6 89 99 71 28

# ÎLE-DE-FRANCE

## LA ROCHE-GUYON

**Official website**
www.larocheguyon.fr/index.html

**Tourist office of the Val d'Oise**
www.valdoise-tourisme.com
Tel.: + 33 (0)1 30 73 39 20

**Château of La Roche-Guyon
and the vegetable garden**
1 Rue de l'Audience
95780 La Roche-Guyon
www.chateaudelarocheguyon.fr
Tel.: + 33 (0)1 34 79 74 42

**Citizens' banquet**
Every July 14 at the château
of La Roche-Guyon.

**Olivia Destailleurs's pottery workshop**
Charrière des Bois
95780 La Roche-Guyon
www.fairedelapoterie.blogspot.fr
Tel.: + 33 (0)6 20 35 43 17

## MAINCY

**Official website**
www.maincy.com

**Town hall**
Tel.: + 33 (0)1 60 68 17 12

**Château of Vaux-le-Vicomte**
www.vaux-le-vicomte.com
www.maincy.com
Tel.: + 33 (0)1 64 14 41 90

# LANGUEDOC-ROUSSILLON

## SAINT-GUILHEM-LE-DÉSERT

**Tourist office**
www.saintguilhem-valleeherault.fr
Tel.: + 33 (0)4 67 57 58 83

**Hike through the Cirque du Bout
du Monde**
www.sentiers.over-blog.com/
article-18667685.html

**Perfumer Nicholas Jennings –
Parfumerie Sharini**
Atelier des Sens
8 Rue Font-de-Portal
34150 Saint-Guilhem-le-Désert
www.sharini.com
Tel.: + 33 (0)4 67 02 78 86

## VILLEFRANCHE-DE-CONFLENT

**Official website**
www.villefranchedeconflent-tourisme.fr
Tel.: + 33 (0)4 68 96 22 96

**Tourist office**
www.office-de-tourisme-canigou-
fenouilledes.com
Tel.: + 33 (0)4 68 97 04 38

**Visiting the ramparts**
Tel.: + 33 (0)4 68 96 22 96
Tourist information point

**Fort Libéria**
www.fort-liberia.com
Tel.: + 33 (0)4 68 96 34 01

**The yellow tourist train**
www.casteil.fr/train%20jaune.htm
Timetable: telechargement.ter-sncf.
com/Images/Languedoc_Roussillon/
Tridion/FH06_PerpignanLatouV2_tcm-
22-82326.pdf

**Caving in the Grandes Canalettes**
www.3grottes.com/infos-pratiques.html
Tel.: + 33 (0)4 68 05 20 20

# LIMOUSIN

## COLLONGES-LA-ROUGE

**Tourist office**
www.ot-collonges.fr
Tel.: + 33 (0)5 55 25 47 57

**Le Moutardier du Pape** (mustard
maker)
19500 Collonges la Rouge
www.lemoutardierdupape.com/fr/
informations.htm
Tel.: + 33 (0)5 55 25 41 00
No restaurant facilities

## TURENNE

**Tourist office**
www.turenne.fr
www.brive-tourisme.com/turenne
Tel.: + 33 (0)5 55 24 08 80

**L'Échoppe à Doudou**
Regional produce for sale.
Place de la Halle
Tel.: + 33 (0)5 55 22 05 28

**Château of Turenne**
www.chateau-turenne.com
Tel.: + 33 (0)5 55 85 90 66
Cell: + 33 (0)6 81 59 97 78

# LORRAINE

## RODEMACK

**Tourist office**
www.tourisme-lorraine.
fr/fr/pagetouristique.
asp?IDPAGET=846140557&sX_Menu_
selectedID=
Tel.: + 33 (0)3 82 56 00 02

**Information center (syndicat d'initiative)**
Tel.: + 33 (0)3 82 51 25 50
ot.rodemack.pagesperso-orange.
fr/2008/depart.htm

**Guided tours of the village**
Information center (syndicat d'initiative)
in Rodemack
Tel.: + 33 (0)3 82 51 25 50

**Amis des Vieilles Pierres**
An association for the restoration
of the village.
avp-rodemack.fr

## SAINT-QUIRIN

**Information center (syndicat d'initiative) of Saint-Quirin and the surrounding area, at Donon**
saint.quirin.free.fr/Pages/tourisme-info.
htm
Tel.: + 33 (0)3 87 08 08 56

**Saint-Quirin Club Vosgien**
Walks and hiking: thirteen signposted
walking trails.
Tel.: + 33 (0)3 87 08 68 42
Cell: + 33 (0)6 73 70 58 13
saint.quirin.free.fr/club-vosgien.html

**Fishing** (day, week, or year permits)
Tel.: + 33 (0)3 87 08 08 56
www.pays-sarrebourg.com/poi.html

# MIDI-PYRÉNÉES

## CONQUES

**Tourist office**
www.tourisme-conques.fr
Tel.: + 33 (0)5 65 72 85 00

**Abbey of Sainte-Foy**
www.abbaye-conques.org

**Centre Européen de Conques**
Cultural events, music festivals,
lectures, and exhibitions.
www.centre-europeen.com
Tel.: + 33 (0)5 65 71 24 00

## SAINT-CIRQ-LAPOPIE

**Tourist office**
www.saint-cirqlapopie.com
Tel.: + 33 (0)5 65 31 31 31

**Patrick Vinel (woodturner)**
46330 Saint-Cirq-Lapopie
Tel.: + 33 (0)5 65 31 20 54

**L'Échappée du Lot**
Cruises on the River Lot
(near Saint-Cirq-Lapopie).
46330 Bouzies
www.lot-croisieres.com
Tel.: + 33 (0)5 65 31 72 25

**Walks along the towpath**
Chemin de Halage
www.saint-cirqlapopie.com/detail/7bc0c
e23b2ee6de8c4f9a66e17d5ce7a/301116

# NORD-PAS-
DE-CALAIS

## MAROILLES

**Official website**
www.maroilles.com

**Information center (syndicat d'initiatives)**
Tel.: + 33 (0)3 27 77 08 23

**Ferme Druesnes** (Maroilles
cheesemakers)
1 Ruelle Vendois
59550 Maroilles
www.parc-naturel-avesnois.fr/
blog/2012/12/06/ferme-dRuesnes
Tel.: + 33 (0)3 27 77 71 55

**Hiking**
maroilles59.free.fr/Pdf/F_RdFr061.pdf
maroilles59.free.fr/Pdf/F_RdFr062.pdf

## WISSANT

**Official website**
www.ville-wissant.fr/spip

**Town hall**
Tel.: + 33 (0)3 21 35 91 22

**Association La Deule**
Sea kayaking and surfing.
59000 Lille
www.ladeule.com
Tel.: + 33 (0)3 20 09 13 02
Fax: + 33 (0)3 20 92 31 23

# PAYS-DE-LA-LOIRE

## MONTSOREAU

**Tourist office**
www.saumur.tourisme.com
Tel.: + 33 (0)2 41 51 70 22

**Official website**
www.ville-montsoreau.fr

**Mushroom-growing at Saut-aux-Loups**
www.troglo-sautauxloups.com
Tel.: + 33 (0)2 41 51 70 30

**La Société l'Union**
Demonstrations of the local sport
of *boule de fort*.
15 Place des Diligences
www.ville-montsoreau.fr/version/fr/
decouvrir_loisirs_activites-loisirs.html
By appointment only

**Château of Montsoreau**
Passage du Marquis de Geoffre
49730 Montsoreau
www.chateau-montsoreau.com
Tel.: + 33 (0)2 41 67 12 60

**Boat trips around Montsoreau**
Trips aboard the *Amarante*
or the *Belle Adèle*.
Montsoreau Port or the Cale du Bac
(Candes-Saint-Martin)
37500 Candes-Saint-Martin
www.bateauamarante.com
Tel.: + 33 (0)2 47 95 80 85

## SAINTE-SUZANNE

**Official website**
www.ste-suzanne.fr

**Tourist office for the Coëvrons**
www.coevrons-tourisme.com
Tel.: + 33 (0)2 43 01 43 60

**Château of Sainte-Suzanne**
1 Rue Fouquet-de-la-Varenne
53270 Sainte-Suzanne
www.chateaudesaintesuzanne.fr
Tel.: + 33 (0)2 43 58 13 00

**Dolmen of Les Erves**
Route d'Assé le Bérenger "Les Erves"
53270 Sainte-Suzanne
Tel.: + 33 (0)2 43 01 43 60

**Walking tour of Le Tertre Ganne hill**
53270 Sainte-Suzanne
www.coevrons-tourisme.com
Tel.: + 33 (0)2 43 01 43 60
Fax: + 33 (0)2 43 01 42 12

**Musée de l'Auditoire** (local history museum)
7 Grande Rue
53270 Sainte-Suzanne
www.museeauditoire.jimdo.com
Tel.: + 33 (0)2 43 01 42 65
Fax: + 33 (0)2 43 01 42 65

# PICARDY

## GERBEROY

**Tourist office**
Tel.: + 33 (0)3 44 46 32 20
ot-picardieverte.free.fr
www.gerberoy.fr

**Jardins Henri Le Sidaner**
Gardens laid out by painter
Henri Le Sidaner.
www.lesjardinshenrilesidaner.fr

**Medieval festival**
Held every year in May.
Contact Les Jardins du Vidamé
4 Impasse du Vidamé
Tel.: + 33 (0)3 44 82 45 32

## PARFONDEVAL

**Tourist office**
www.tourisme-thierache.fr/fr

**Town hall**
Tel.: + 33 (0)3 23 97 78 97

**Fortified church of Parfondeval**
www.tourisme-thierache.fr/fr/
Histoire-Patrimoine/Eglise-fortifee-
de-Parfondeval-PARFONDEVAL
Tel.: + 33 (0)3 23 98 50 39
Fax: + 33 (0)3 23 98 87 67
Free entry

**Protestant church**
Tel.: + 33 (0)3 23 97 63 73
Free entry

# POITOU-CHARENTES

## ANGLES-SUR-L'ANGLIN

**Tourist office**
www.anglessuranglin.com
Tel.: + 33 (0)5 49 48 86 87

**Maison des Jours d'Angles
et du Tourisme**
*Jours d'Angles* embroidery.
Tel.: + 33 (0)5 49 48 86 87
Open all year

**Roc-aux-Sorciers**
Interpretation Center for
the Magdalenian paintings
in the Roc-aux-Sorciers.
2 Route des Certeaux
86260 Angles-sur-l'Anglin
www.roc-aux-sorciers.com
Tel.: + 33 (0)5 49 83 37 27
(between 9.30 a.m. and 6 p.m.)

**Château**
Tel.: + 33 (0)5 49 48 61 20
Free entry

## TALMONT-SUR-GIRONDE

**Official website**
www.talmont-sur-gironde.fr

**Town hall**
Tel.: + 33 (0)5 46 90 43 87

**Musée de l'Histoire Locale
et de la Pêche** (museum of local
history and fishing)
Tel.: + 33 (0)5 46 96 17 85
Guided museum tours from April
to September

**Guided tours around the village**
Tel.: + 33 (0)5 46 96 17 85

# PROVENCE-ALPES-
CÔTE D'AZUR

## LES BAUX-DE-PROVENCE

**Tourist office**
www.lesbauxdeprovence.com
Tel.: + 33 (0)4 90 54 34 39

**Château of Les Baux**
www.chateau-baux-provence.com
Tel.: + 33 (0)4 90 54 55 56

**Val d'Enfer trail**
Tel.: + 33 (0)4 90 54 34 39 (tourist office)

## MOUSTIERS-SAINTE-MARIE

**Tourist office**
www.moustiers.eu
Tel.: + 33 (0)4 92 74 67 84

**Atelier Bondil** (artisan potter)
Rue de la Bourgade
www.faiencebondil.fr

**L'Etoile nautical center**
www.etoile.moustiers.fr
Tel.: + 33 (0)4 94 70 22 48

**La Cadeno sailing club**
www.lacadeno.fr
Tel.: + 33 (0)4 92 72 56 60

**La Bastide de Moustiers**
Hotel and restaurant run
by Alain Ducasse.
Chemin de Quinson
04360 Moustiers-Sainte-Marie
www.bastide-moustiers.com
Tel.: + 33 (0)4 92 70 47 47

# RHÔNE-ALPES

## PÉROUGES

**Tourist office**
www.perouges.org
Tel.: + 33 (0)4 74 46 70 84

**Guided tours around the village**
www.perouges.org
Book online

## YVOIRE

**Tourist office**
www.yvoiretourism.com/accueil_fr.html
Tel.: + 33 (0)4 50 72 80 21

**Jardin des Cinq Sens**
("Garden of the Five Senses")
www.jardin5sens.net

**Art et Vannerie**
The last basket maker in Haute-Savoie.
Rue de l'Église
74140 Yvoire
www.yvoiretourism.com/chapitre5_
fr_3_54.html
Tel.: + 33 (0)6 80 90 79 53

# INDEX OF THE
# BEST LOVED VILLAGES
# OF FRANCE

**Acknowledgments**

This book would never have been possible without the combined talents
of Stéphane Bern and Morgane Production.

The publisher would like to thank France Télévisions and all those who took part in the project,
and first and foremost Françoise Fonquernie for her invaluable collaboration.

Morgane Production expresses its gratitude to all the mayors and tourist offices concerned for their warm welcome,
and to the villages' inhabitants, who often acted as "guides for a day."

Special appreciation goes to Gilles Hardeveld, mayor of Saint-Cirq-Lapopie,
and to Claude Centlivre, mayor of Eguisheim.

Morgane Production would like to thank all the wonderful teams at France 2,
France Télévisions Distribution, France Télévisions Numérique,
and especially Nathalie André, Nicolas Marinos, Philippe Vilamitjana, Perrine Fontaine,
Antoine Boilley, Philippe Landré, Emmanuelle Guilcher, Yann Chapellon, Joseph Jacquet,
Caroline Scherrer, Ségolène Zaug, and Pierre-Jean Meurine.

Morgane Production would like to express its particular thanks to Stéphane Bern,
France's favorite television presenter!

# Photographic Credits

(c: center; t: top; b: bottom; r: right; l: left)

The images reproduced on pp. 18l, 44bl, 48t, 68b, 73r, 91tr, 100t, 105b, 111t, 131tr, 142b, 181r, 190bl,
and 216br are all stills from the television program *Le Village préféré des Français*, broadcast by France Télévisions,
and devised and produced by Morgane Production.
The photograph on p. 58tl is copyright © Les anis de Flavigny.


The remainder of the photographs are courtesy of HEMIS photo agency.
The first independent French photo agency to specialize in images of tourism and discovery,
HEMIS (www.hemis.fr) has become a benchmark in the fields of book and magazine publishing, corporate communication,
and advertising thanks to a database of some twenty million pictures.
The agency promotes the work of talented travel, lifestyle, nature, animal,
and art photographers from France and the rest of the world.


**G. Antoni**: 97c. **J.-P. Azam**: 23br, 151, 155br, 172br, 173, 174t, 174br, 176b, 180br. **B. Barbier**: 161c.
**J.-M. Barrere**: 28, 29t, 29b, 30t, 30b, 31t, 31b, 136. **E. Berthier**: 67c, 67b, 68–69, 69b, 71l, 73l, 74tl, 74tr.
**P. Body**: 26, 27tl, 27tr, 76, 78–79, 79t, 80b, 81t, 81b, 84t, 84br, 195bl, 195br, 196t, 196b, 198–199t, 199bl, 199tr, 200,
201t, 201b, 218, 219bl, 222. **C. Boisvieux**: 54, 55b, 58r, 71r, 99, 100b, 101t, 104. **D. Bringard**: 160. **M. Cavalier**: 224.
**D. Caviglia**: 14t, 15, 23bl, 55t, 56, 57, 59t, 60br, 61, 102b, 166, 166l, 166r, 168, 169t, 169b, 232, 233tr. **F. Charton**: 106.
**A. Chicurel**: 24–25, 62–63, 129c, 132, 134t, 194–195t, 203c, 212. **R. Cintract**: 31b. **M. Colin**: 98b. **S. Cordier**: 225b.
**F. Cormon**: 43c, 43br, 46–47, 48b, 119t, 119b, 120r, 120l, 121, 129b, 131tl, 131bl, 165b. **J.-P. Degas**: 127c, 137b, 161b, 197.
**Y. Doelan**: 225t. **J. Du Boisberranger**: 143b. **P. Escudero**: 22, 77c, 88, 89t, 89b, 90, 91tl, 91br, 171c, 182, 213t, 213c.
**J.-P. Forget**: 118. **P. Frilet**: 72, 75. **B. Gardel**: 127c. **G. Gerault**: 53b, 107c, 107b, 110. **L. Giraudou**: 11t, 237t. **M. Gotin**: 43t.
**F. Guiziou**: 87t, 107t, 108, 109l, 109r, 112–113, 112bl, 112br, 114, 115t, 137t, 142t, 143t, 144, 145tr, 145b, 146t, 147, 149t, 170, 171b, 227b,
230bl, 231, 238, 239l, 239r, 240t, 240bl, 240br, 241, 246tl, 246tr. **C. Guy**: 77b, 148, 149c, 149b, 155t, 155bl, 157bl, 157br, 159t.
**R. Harding**: 55c. **C. Heeb**: 66. **P. Houze**: 186t, 235tr. **H. Hughes**: 42, 155b, 177t, 163tr. **P. Jacques**: 137c, 138, 175, 178–179,
226, 228–229, 230r, 236, 242–243t, 243b, 244–245, 246br, 247. **Jon Arnold**: 17, 43b, 49b, 101b, 111b, 183c. **A. Kauffmann**: 203b.
**S. Lemaire**: 98t, 102–103, 172bl, 174bl. **H. Lenain**: 27b, 50–51t, 51b, 52l, 52r, 53t, 64t, 64b, 65, 80t, 150tl, 150tr, 152–153t, 154, 156–157t,
158t, 158b, 176–177t, 177b, 193c, 214, 216bl, 216tr, 223t, 223bl, 223br, 233tl, 235l. **F. Leroy**: 82t, 82b, 83, 146b, 192, 193b, 215, 220–221.
**J.-P. Lescourret**: 9c. **L. Maisant**: 64c. **R. Mattes**: 8, 9t, 10–11, 14b, 16t, 16b, 18, 19t, 19b, 105t, 162–163t, 163bl, 164t, 164b, 165t.
**C. Moirenc**: 87b, 96, 97t, 190t, 225c, 234, 235br, 237b. **P. Moulu**: 131br, 204–205, 206, 207tl, 207tr, 207br, 208, 209l, 209r, 210, 211t, 211b.
**J.-B. Rabouan**: 77t. **B. Rieger**: 11b, 12–13, 44–45, 59b, 70, 74b, 84bl, 92l, 92r, 93, 94, 95t, 95b, 116, 177b, 122t, 122b, 123, 124l, 124r, 125,
127b, 128, 130, 133t, 133b, 134b, 135, 140–141, 219br, 230tl. **G. Rigoulet**: 49t, 177c, 190br. **P. Roy**: 193t, 237c.
**C. Sarramon**: 180bl. **A. Serrano**: 126. **R. Soberka**: 87c, 183t, 184–185t, 186b, 187t, 187bl, 187br, 188, 189, 191tl, 191tr, 202.
**S. Sonnet**: 60bl, 141r. **B. Stichelbaut**: 67t. **J.-D. Sudres**: 9b, 20, 21t, 21c, 21b, 29b, 30b, 86, 103b, 145tl, 159b, 161t,
171t, 181, 183b, 185b, 203t, 213b, 216. **E. Suetone**: 97b.


**hemis·fr**
TRAVELS LIFESTYLE | MAGES